Modernization and Development

The Search for Alternative Paradigms

THE UNITED NATIONS UNIVERSITY

STUDIES ON SOCIO-CULTURAL DEVELOPMENT ALTERNATIVES IN A CHANGING WORLD
General Editor: Anouar Abdel-Malek

The United Nations University's Project on Socio-cultural Development Alternatives in a Changing World (SCA), 1978-1982, arose from the deeply felt need to re-posit the problematique of human and social development in view of the dominant, Western-centred, reductionist models of development. The study concentrated on two major dimensions, constituting two sub-projects – Endogenous Intellectual Creativity and Transformation of the World – while select major thematic, innovative Convergence Areas (e.g., specificity and universality, geo-cultural visions of the world) were explored. Under the former theme development and its related issues were examined in terms of different geo-cultural areas of the world: Asia, Africa, the Arab World, Latin America, Europe, and North America. Under the latter sub-project consideration was given to the analysis of world transformation in the domains of science and technology, economy and society, culture and thought, religion and philosophy, and the making of a new international order.

The SCA series includes reports on collective research undertaken, its results and orientations, and theoretical studies on select themes, all aimed at the formulation of more realistic and sophisticated policies concerning the complex issue of development alternatives in a changing world.

TITLES IN THIS SERIES

Partha Chatterjee
Nationalist Thought and the Colonial World: A Derivative Discourse?
1986

S.C. Dube
Modernization and Development: The Search for Alternative Paradigms
1988

Tamas Szentes
The Transformaton of the World Economy: New Directions and New Interests?
1988

THE UNITED NATIONS UNIVERSITY

STUDIES ON SOCIO-CULTURAL DEVELOPMENT
ALTERNATIVES IN A CHANGING WORLD

Modernization and Development

The Search for Alternative Paradigms

S.C. Dube

The United Nations University
Tokyo

Zed Books Ltd
London and New Jersey

Modernization and Development: The Search for Alternative Paradigms was first published in 1988
by
Zed Books Ltd, 57 Caledonian Road, London N1 9BU, UK, and
171 First Avenue, Atlantic Highlands, New Jersey 07716, USA
and
The United Nations University, Toho Seimei Building,
15-1 Shibuya 2-chome, Shibuya-ku, Tokyo 150, Japan.

Copyright © The United Nations University, 1988.

Cover designed by Lee Robinson.
Printed and bound in the United Kingdom
at The Bath Press, Avon.

British Library Cataloguing in Publication Data

Dube, S.C.
   Modernization and development : the
   search for alternative paradigms.——(Socio-
   cultural development alternatives in a
   changing world).
   1. Social change   2. Economic development
   I. Title   II. Series
   361.6   HM101

   ISBN 0-86232-728-8
   ISBN 0-86232-729-6 Pbk

Library of Congress Cataloging-in-Publication Data

Dube, S.C. (Shyama Charan), 1922—
   Modernization and development : the search for alternative
paradigms / S.C. Dube.

      p.   cm.——(Socio-cultural development alternatives in a
changing world)
      ISBN 0-86232-728-8 : $39.95 (U.S.). ISBN 0-86232-729-6 (pbk.) :
$12.50 (U.S.)
      1. Economic development. 2. Economic development—Environmental
aspects. 3. Economic development—Social aspects. 4. Quality of
life. I. Title. II. Series.
HD87.D8   1988
338.9——dc19

Contents

Preface and Acknowledgements

This book is the outcome of a project on "rethinking development" on which I am working as a National Fellow of the Indian Council of Social Sciences Research. Limited in its scope and practical in its orientation, it attempts a review of development thinking and practice, seeks to examine the paradigm shift and the emergence of an alternative model, and focuses on the ambiguities, ambivalences and contradictions in the praxis of planning, economic growth and directed social change. It deliberately avoids abstract philosophical speculation and sophisticated model building. The book is not addressed primarily to the world of scholarship: I have in view a readership of policy makers, planners and thinking and concerned individuals. Many ideas incorporated in this volume have been developed in several of my previous papers and some will find elucidation and elaboration in forthcoming contributions.

This book was to have been written in collaboration with my wife, Professor Leela Dube. The format was planned jointly by us; but both being constantly on the move and together only for limited periods, only one of us could write the book. With her many other commitments Leela Dube withdrew from the assignment, leaving the responsibility for completing the task to me.

I am indebted to many institutions and individuals, but can acknowledge only a few by name. The first in the list is the Indian Council of Social Science Research, which invited me to accept its National Fellowship so that I could be relieved of the arduous responsibilities of the vice-chancellorship of a university and devote myself full-time to reflection and writing. The National Institute of Educational Planning and Administration provided me with a cosy base and many amenities so that I could work in reasonable comfort. At the United Nations Asian and Pacific Development Centre (APDC) I was extended every help in completing this work alongside the other responsibilities that I had to take on as a consultant. I am indebted for the institutional support given by the Indian Council of Social Science Research, and the National Institute of Educational Planning and Administration, both in New Delhi, and the United Nations Asian and Pacific Development Centre, Kuala Lumpur.

The list of persons to whom I am indebted for criticism, comment and emotional support is indeed long. Mr Aftab Ahmad Khan, a brilliant and widely experienced civil servant from Pakistan and Director of the United Nations Asian and Pacific Development Centre, evinced keen interest in the completion of this volume. He has read every chapter of the book and his perceptive comments inform several of the ideas developed here. His experience in Pakistan, the Gulf countries and with the World Bank provided many invaluable insights. Above everything else, I cherish his gift of friendship. Also at the United Nations Asian and Pacific Development Centre I had many discussions with Dr Ahmad Fattahipour on the theme of the book and on other related matters. Two other professionals who have read early drafts of the work and commented on them are Professor Leela Dube of the Institute of Development Studies, Jaipur, and Professor Yogesh Atal, Regional Adviser for Social Sciences, UNESCO, Bangkok. My relationship with them precludes me from thanking them formally.

The comprehensive bibliography to the volume was prepared by Ms Agnes How with the collaboration of Ms Siti Rafeah Shamsuddin. It is based largely on the bibliography prepared by the APDC library for the Conference on Development Perspectives for the 1980s organized by the United Nations Asian and Pacific Development Centre in December 1981; parts not relevant have been deleted, additional entries have been made and several sections have been specially prepared for this study. Agnes How has been a warm friend and a gracious hostess. Ng Get Meng, also of the APDC library, has constantly provided me with additional references and photocopies of urgently needed articles. At the National Institute of Educational Planning and Administration, New Delhi, Ms Nizmad Malhatza placed her considerable library resources at my disposal. My thanks to all.

Early drafts of three of the chapters were prepared in India where Mr Harish Bhatia provided efficient stenographic assistance. They were rewritten and the rest of the chapters were newly written at the United Nations Asian and Pacific Development Centre. Without the ungrudging, willing and concerned cooperation of Ms Shaleha Haron it would have been impossible for me to complete the work speedily. Ms Haron was a secretary, a research and reference assistant, and more. Formal words of thanks cannot adequately express what I owe to her.

Finally, my thanks to Professor Anouar Abdel-Malek, Project Coordinator, United Nations University Project on *Socio-Cultural Development Alternatives in a Changing World* (SCA) for all his kindness and consideration.

S.C. Dube

1 Dilemmas of Modernization and Development

Two Keywords

Modernization and development have come to be keywords in the contemporary dialogue on the human condition. Though the two have a different intellectual ancestry, through a process of redefinition of objectives as well as conceptual and methodological convergence, they have come close to each other in substantive meaning. They share three reference points. First, they refer to the states of society. Theorists of modernization distinguish between *traditional*, *transitional* and *modernized* societies. Development theorists, on the other hand, speak of *underdeveloped*, *developing*, and *developed* societies. Second, both of them articulate a set of goals in the sense that the ideal of modernization or development provides an agenda for action. Third, both the concepts refer to a process – movement from tradition to modernity or from underdevelopment to development. The criteria that determine the state of societies are value loaded in the sense that they mainly take into account the volume of GNP and degree of industrialization. These criteria apply also to the set of goals; sights were set rather high when developing societies uncritically accepted the development theorists' assumption that life begins at $1,000 per capita and when an economic historian of Rostow's repute suggested that the test of development is one car for four persons in the society. With the wisdom gained from the experience of the last three decades a greater degree of realism has been introduced into the setting of goals which, in proximate terms, are now confined to meeting basic needs and to the gradual upgrading of the quality of life. The complexity and inherent difficulties of the process of modernization are now better understood and appreciated. Simplistic unilinear theories indicating essential stages and steps towards the realization of modernity or development no longer carry much conviction. The models of the processes leading to modernization and economic growth/development have undergone significant modifications. The modernization paradigm, built upon interdisciplinary perspectives from the behavioural sciences, now has a better appreciation of economic imperatives. Development economics, in turn, shows greater sensitivity to the behavioural and institutional aspects of development.

The fusion of the two concepts, however, has not so far taken place. Semantic differences still persist, as do differences in emphasis. Yet there is unmistakable evidence of greater convergence and a cross-fertilization of the ideas implicit in the two concepts.

Mental attitudes and institutional structures constitute the key elements in the process of modernization. James O'Connell (1976, p. 17) has a very apt expression to describe the essence of the modernization process.[1] He calls it *creative rationality*. Combining the concepts of innovation and order, this mental attitude begins to develop once the modernization process has taken off. He identifies three connected and interactive aspects that are basic to the process. In his words, they are: (1) a tested conviction of the existence of correlations and causes that maintains a continuing, systematic and inventive search for knowledge – in other words, an analytico–causal and inventive outlook; (2) the multiplication of tools and techniques that both results from the first aspect and nourishes it; and (3) a willingness to accept continuous change on the plane of both individual and social structures, together with a capacity meanwhile to preserve individual and social identity.

A series of societal changes are implicit in the process of modernization. Traditional agrarian societies are characterized by the predominance of ascriptive, particularistic and diffused patterns; they have stable local groups and limited spatial mobility; occupational differentiation is relatively simple and stable; and the stratification system is deferential and has a diffused impact. The modern industrial society, on the other hand, is characterized by the predominance of universalistic, specific and achievement norms; a high degree of mobility; a developed occupational system relatively insulated from other social structures; a class system based generally on achievement; and the presence of functionally specific, non-ascriptive structures (associations). Historically evolved institutions continuously adapt themselves to the changes dictated by the phenomenal increases in human knowledge that have resulted from the greater control of humanity over its environment. Modernization theory does not clearly spell out its distributive objectives; but the emergence of an implicit egalitarian and participative ethos does indicate the narrowing of social gaps and promotion of greater equality as desirable ends.

The notion of development in early economics was simple and uninvolved. Development meant the capacity of static national economies to generate and sustain an annual increase in their Gross National Product at the rates of 5% to 7% or more. The decade of the 1960s was designated by the UN as the "Development Decade"; the target laid down for the period was the attainment of 6% annual growth rate of GNP. Another indicator used by economists was the relationship between the growth of per capita GNP and the ability of a nation to expand its output at a rate faster than the growth rate of its population. Rates and levels of growth of *real* per capita GNP were also calculated to determine the degree of economic development. In such calculations the rate of price inflation was deducted from the monetary growth of GNP per capita. Such a notion of economic development aimed at a planned alteration of the structure of production and employment. The size and share of the rural agricultural sector was to decline; those of the urban industrial sector, involving the growth of manufacturing and service industries, were assumed to expand progressively. Non-economic social indicators of development were touched upon only in passing. The trickle down effect of overall per capita GNP growth was expected to provide more jobs and economic opportunities, ensuring wider diffusion of the benefits of growth.

But in the developing countries things did not work out the way the economists had predicted. The "invisible hand" (a term originating in Adam Smith's *Wealth of Nations*, written in 1776) did not wave a magic wand. The social benefits of growth remained confined to small sections of the population, without reaching down to the person in the street. It was increasingly felt that getting the growth job done was not enough. Hence economic development was redefined and related to the objectives of the elimination of poverty, inequality and unemployment within the framework of a growing economy. In the process redistribution was inevitably linked to growth. Three core values were gradually incorporated in the notion of development: life sustenance, self-esteem and freedom of choice.

Many vital questions related to both modernization and development continue to exercise development thinkers and planners. Definitive answers to them are yet to be found.

Nature of Modernization and Development

In his perceptive essay, "The Change to Change: Modernization, Development, and Politics," Samuel P. Huntington (1976, pp. 30–31) has identified nine characteristics of the modernization process which, according to him, are generally agreed upon by scholars.[2] These characteristics are applicable equally to the process of development.

1. Modernization, and by implication development, is a revolutionary process. Its technological and cultural consequences are as significant as those of the Neolithic Revolution which turned food gathering and hunting nomads into settled agriculturalists. Efforts are now being made to transform rural agrarian cultures into urban industrial cultures. This is what Alvin Toffler (1980) would describe as the move from the first wave to the second wave.[3]

H: modernization = development

* *The change to change: Mod. Dev., and politics*
4: Modernization = Neolithic Revolution

2. The process of both modernization and development are complex and multidimensional. They involve a series of cognitive, behavioural and institutional modifications and restructuring.

3. Both are systemic processes. Variation in one dimension produces important covariations in other dimensions.

4. They are global processes. Ideas and techniques are diffused from the centre of origination to other parts of the world.

5. They are lengthy processes. Time is important in both modernization and development. There are no known methods of producing them instantly.

6. They are phased processes. Historical experience indicates that the movement towards the goals of modernization and development takes place through identifiable phases and sub-phases.

7. They are homogenizing processes. As modernization and development move to advanced stages differences between national societies are narrowed and ultimately a stage is reached when the "universal imperative of modern ideas and institutions prevail, leading to a point at which the various societies are so homogenized as to be capable of forming a world state" (Black, 1966, pp. 155, 174).[4]

8. Both are irreversible processes. There is no going back from modernization and development, although there may be occasional upsets and temporary breakdowns.

9. They are progressive processes. Modernization and development are inevitable as well as desirable. In the long run they contribute to human well-being both culturally and materially.

There can be little dispute about the processes of modernization and development being revolutionary, complex, systemic, lengthy and phased. It is open to serious question, however, whether they are global. Some benefits of modernization and development have been widely diffused, but a large section of humankind remains untouched by them. The contradictions implicit in the process leave it to be doubted whether the ideal of equal modernization and development on a global scale can ever materialize. Given the present trends it looks most unlikely. When one small section of mankind, in Toffler's metaphor (1980), is moving from the second to the third wave, two-thirds of humankind is constrained by the conspiracy of circumstances to remain a part of the first wave.[5] The growing disparities make nonsense of the global dimension of modernization and development, except in the very limited sense that all societies are trying to modernize and develop.

The homogenization aspect raises some further fundamental questions. It is common these days to describe the world as a global village, but we must take account of the rise and gathering strength of ethnicities and pluralities of culture consciousness that are tearing it apart. The manner in which the superpowers behave does not augur well for any meaningful global homogenization. The developing countries have also been drawn into the whirlpool of tension and conflict and their differences are posing a threat to world peace. Whether the process is irreversible, time alone will show. At this stage we can only take note of the rise of fundamentalism in many societies and the strength that counter-modernization and counter-development ideologies have gained in many others. It is a matter of opinion and cultural valuation whether modernization and development are progressive. Doubtless the benefits conferred by them are substantial; but the social cost and cultural erosion implicit in them is also considerable. Several trends visible in the more developed countries cannot by any means be described as progressive. There is growing evidence of individual alienation and social anomie. Individual and collective violence is increasing. The normative structure of society is becoming weak and many social institutions are becoming dysfunctional. These countries find it difficult to hold such trends in check. This is what necessitates rethinking the objectives and strategies of modernization and development. Some of their injuries are avoidable; less injurious and more equitable paths to development and modernization can be found. This is what the debate on alternatives is about. The future of modernization and development depends, in the final analysis, on how humanity handles the present state of international disorder and global maldistribution of resources. If the superpowers take the collision course and reject the logic of the projected New International Economic Order the future – if there is one – remains bleak.

In retrospect three more characteristics of modernization and development can be identified. First, it should be recognized that they are painful processes. Modernization and development have previously been built on considerable exploitation of certain segments of the society and have involved a degree of ruthlessness. Imperialism aided them substantially. Their astonishing accomplishments have caused and are still causing considerable social injuries. They have resulted in international as well as intranational duality. The nations of the world can be divided between the privileged and the underprivileged, the number of the former being much smaller. Intranationally a similar duality prevails. In most countries there is a small privileged group surrounded by a large mass of underprivileged. Attempted justifications of the inevitability of this injury-causing dimension of the process were made in the initial phases, though not necessarily by those whom it hurt. Now it is being openly challenged.

Second, modernization and development are multilinear/multipath processes. Recent historical experience suggests that all societies do not necessarily have to take the same road to modernization and development; alternative paths can be followed.

Third, neither can be visualized as continuous and unending. They are conditioned by "outer" and "inner" limits. Human perceptions can change, and are changing, the finalities and the course of modernization and development.

Debate in Disarray

The gap between the promise and performance of development and modernization during the last three decades has caused acute disappointment which, in its turn, has led to heart searching. Many different diagnoses have been offered; linked to them is an equally bewildering number and variety of suggested remedies. Not only development, but the *debate* on development is in disarray. In the cacophony of ideas and strategies the Third World seems lost. A viable and sustainable approach is not yet within sight. None the less, the debate must continue.

Let us consider some of the dilemmas of development – the major issues and options under discussion.

The first dilemma concerns development vs non-development. The disenchantment with the outcome of the development effort of the last thirty years is so great that many serious thinkers in the Third World have begun to regard development as Enemy Number One of humankind and have become the devotees of non-development. The zero-rate-of-growth ideology is not a gimmick; to some it is an article of faith. It is true that the promised pay-off of development has not come about and that both its performance and non-performance have generated a series of intractable problems. Governments are finding it increasingly hard to cope with these problems; but the non-development ideology as a remedy may be worse than the disease. The phenomenal population explosion; acute shortage of food, energy, and other natural resources and their maldistribution; and the serious threats to the environment are problems that cannot be left to resolve themselves. They pose a challenge and call for a conscious and determined intervention in the processes of history.

The second dilemma is that of endogenous vs exogenous development. One of the paradoxes of the modern world is that while its constituent societies are getting potentially closer to one another, this centripetal tendency is obstructed by the simultaneous operation of centrifugal forces rooted in ethnicity, religion, culture and language. According to one estimate, the world is currently witnessing over 370 movements of varying strengths rooted in diverse interpretations of the concept of ethnicity. The cultural reality of developing societies cannot be brushed aside; all efforts at development have to be sensitive and responsive to it. The objectives of development will be considerably influenced by endogenous factors. At the same time, the reality of the diffusion of ideas and innovations as a force in humanity's cultural development cannot be denied. Both transcend national boundaries; but ideas, institutions and technology have to be adapted to the endogenous ethos. No society can remain totally uninfluenced by exogenous factors. The compulsions of the situation require a mix of the two.

Self-reliance vs interdependence in development pose the third dilemma which, in recent discussions, has been formulated as inward-looking vs outward-looking development. Countries differ in the size of their territory and population as well as in their physical resources endowment. Large countries such as China and India can and have been aiming at a high degree of self-reliance; but even they cannot hope to be totally self-reliant. Smaller countries, especially island societies and landlocked nations, cannot achieve the same degree of self-reliance. They have to look for both capital and technology, as well as some natural resources, elsewhere. While a self-reliant and inward-looking approach to development has some advantages, no society can afford to become insular. Patterns of interdependence – sub-regional, regional and global – have to be developed. What has to be guarded against is this interdependence turning into a patron–client relationship which results in the subordination and dependency of the Third World country.

The attitude of the affluent countries to development aid has often been cynical, if not downright perverse. Recall, for example, the dilemma of triage vs aid to the neediest. It was seriously suggested that some societies were incapable of utilizing the aid extended to them and that any assistance to them only went into a bottomless pit, without producing any positive results. Help should be rendered only to those capable of using it, others should be left to fend for themselves – however dire the consequences. Aid has its cost and cannot be relied on.

The fourth major dilemma, which has been resolved at the conceptual level but not at the operational level, relates to growth vs distribution. In contemporary development thinking GNP has been dethroned because it has proved inadequate to produce equity and social justice. The current emphasis is on redistribution aimed at meeting basic needs, providing employment and improving social services. The central question, however, still remains unanswered: without growth, what will the societies have to distribute? The growth factor cannot be ignored, although its distributional dimension must constantly be emphasized.

The next set of dilemmas relate to different dimensions of centralized planning. The first of them can be formulated as centralized planning vs the operation of the market. Should the targets be decided by a central planning agency? Or should market mechanisms and price signals be left free to shape and reshape them? It is clear that the magic of the market place has not proved very effective in the context of the developing societies and that price signals have often been manipulated and therefore found misleading. It has to be noted, however, that even the centrally planned economies are showing increasing sensitivity to the price signals. The latter cannot be ignored so long as the world remains divided between free market and centrally planned economies. The second dilemma in this context is one of the intranational centralization vs the decentralization of planning; closely related to it is the dilemma of mass participation vs professionalism. The conditions prevailing in most Third World countries require a strong centre; but this argument does not even remotely imply segregation of the planners from those for whom planning is carried out. It is necessary to allow the people access to planning decentralization. This, along with mass partici-pation, would reflect local and regional needs better and would ensure greater and more effective mobilization of human resources. A high degree of professionalism is necessary, but it is well to remember that bureaucracy and professional planners have both trained incompetence as well as trained competence. People must remain the masters.

Several dilemmas of an operational nature, involving choosing the right options, can be considered together. The first of these can be posed as one of industrialization vs the environment. The environmental threat posed by developed societies is greater than that posed by less developed societies. Pollution, as well as pollution-causing technology is exported by developed societies to the less developed. The more industrialized societies will, therefore, need to give serious consideration to earmarking part of their GNP for the research and development that will ensure a technology that produces minimal pollution, no wasteful consumption of scarce and non-renewable resources and conservation and improvement of the environment. At the same time they should ensure that they do not export to the Third World a technology that leads to high pollution and requires wasteful expenditure of energy and natural resources. On its part, the Third World should resist the import of such technology.

It would be absurd to advise the Third World not to industrialize for the sake of the environment. The environmental problems of the less developed countries are of a different order altogether. As Indira Gandhi has rightly said, for these societies poverty is the greatest pollutant. Removal of poverty will significantly contribute to improvements in the quality of environment. Environmental consciousness, however, has to be promoted in these societies so that they do not encounter problems of unmanageable proportions later. It should be noted that greed and lack of foresight have been responsible for considerable environmental degradation in the Third World; this must be reversed.

The dilemmas of industry vs agriculture, import substitution vs export promotion, aid vs trade, free international trade vs regional integration and protection have been much debated and need not detain us long. These do not necessarily pose either/or choices; a judicious combination of both is to be attempted. Agricultural production has to be emphasized; but experience suggests that in many Third World countries production is maintained at satisfactory levels – it is the system of distribution that goes wrong. The delivery system is defective. But more important than that is the fact that while there is enough food to go round, the majority have such low purchasing power that they cannot obtain sufficient food to meet their nutritional needs. In any case no one can seriously recommend perpetuation of two separate worlds, one mainly agrarian, the other mainly industrial. To the extent that it is possible Third World countries will have to adopt a policy of import substitution; but this policy may not work in respect of all the items needed for development. The global distribution of natural resources is uneven and unequal, necessitating imports of at least some essential items. In any event, efforts at import substitution and export promotion can go together, although the latter has to face several visible and invisible barriers.

The question of aid vs trade is tricky. Aid rarely comes without stringent conditions attached to it. Much of it is in support of projects and the package deal is often as, if not more, advantageous to the aid giver than it is to the aid-receiver. In fact, the term aid is a misnomer; loans that have to be repaid with interest can hardly be described as aid. The burden of international loans is sometimes so heavy that a substantial part of subsequent borrowings goes into debt servicing. It is undeniable that many forms of aid are exploitative; some are barely disguised imperialism. An inward looking view of development, therefore, would seek to do away with aid from the affluent countries as soon as possible, although some aid may be necessary for some time. Trade is also on unequal terms. What the more developed countries require are raw materials and semi-processed goods. Protectionism and tariff barriers hinder export promotion and trade. The entire question of trade between the more developed and less developed countries requires a careful review and urgent measures of rectification. Intra-Third World patterns of commodity exchange and trade will have to be evolved, taking care that the terms are fair and just.

Let us turn briefly to the dilemma of physical investment vs investment in human capital and to two important problems associated with it. Evidently physical input is necessary but much of it will go to waste if the human resources for its proper utilization are not there. Thus, investment in human capital has an edge over physical investment. It can be argued that human resources alone can achieve little if the necessary physical inputs for development are absent. There is considerable force in this argument. What is necessary, therefore, is to work for the right mix of investment in human capital and physical investment. Human resources can be enriched by raising and enlarging consciousness and by developing trained competence and skills through education. This brings us to the dilemmas of formal vs non-formal education and schooling vs deschooling. The dichotomy between formal and non-formal education is, in a sense, unreal; both are needed and both have specific functions. According a low priority to formal education is likely to widen the knowledge gap between the more developed and the less developed countries. It will result in a scientific and technological lag; the Third World will have lost the opportunity and hope of catching up with the developed world in these spheres. Quality and excellence, therefore, will have to be pursued through formal channels of education. At the same time removal of mass illiteracy will require experiments with non-formal methods of education. Programmes of adult education and extension education will have to be promoted. The non-formal channel can also be used to impart and upgrade various kinds of skills required for the development endeavour. The deschooling doctrine is founded on valid and well argued social criticism; but it does not offer any positive leads. The entire structure of education, including its objectives and instrumentalities, needs a careful examination. It has carry overs from the colonial past and in several aspects it is irrelevant. This requires correction. Deschooling under a myopic political leadership and hamhanded bureaucracy can, however, prove to be an unmitigated disaster.

The dilemma of the latest technology vs intermediate/appropriate technology impinges both on physical investment and investment in human capital. The Third World cannot opt permanently for low technology. This would lead yet again to the perpetuation of the great divide between the more developed and the less developed. However, the type of technology that a country adopts should not be made a matter of prestige; technology should be needs specific. In the initial stages a great deal of it will have to be labour-intensive and not capital-intensive, but there are certain areas where adopting the latest technology is unavoidable. Small may be beautiful, but it does not always work and it does not solve all problems. Therefore, depending on the nature of the activity, a country would have to choose from high, medium and low technology. Two considerations in this respect are paramount. Technology must function as an instrument in the service of humanity and not the reverse. Second, the less developed countries must not be persuaded to choose options that will relegate them to permanently retarded scientific and technological positions.

Then there is the great debate around the dilemma of evolutionary vs revolutionary development. Much depends on how revolution is defined. History suggests that transformations with a revolutionary impact have taken place in the course of normal evolution. But revolution, as a means of last resort, should not be ruled out if societies fail to resolve their inner contradiction and fail to evolve an equitable redistribution pattern. At the same time it should be borne in mind that revolution is not magic. It has its social costs and injuries. It involves careful planning, successful mobilization and dedicated hard work. Achieving a real revolution is much more difficult than radical rhetoric or postures. A revolution which fails can only mean chaos. Under certain circumstances it may be necessary and even inevitable; but the demands that it makes in terms of organization and sacrifices should always be kept in mind.

Finally, to the dilemma of one development vs many developments. Is development a unilinear process leading humanity to a common destiny? Or are several developments following multilinear paths, each with a different set of objectives and strategies, possible? The one development model has several ambiguities and inadequacies. Depending upon cultural specificities several developments, each informed and inspired by endogenous creativity, are possible. Cultural diversity will always exist. Rather than thinking in terms of one universal developmental design, it is useful to contemplate the possibility of several possible futures and designs for living.

Towards the 21st Century

It is sobering to reflect on the performance of modernization; contemplation of its future is chilling. As we move slowly towards the 21st Century, some gruesome aspects of the future impinge, reminding *homo sapiens* that he has not been very wise after all. An architect of majestic and mighty civilization and the performer of breathtaking feats in the field of science and technology, the human animal finds itself helpless and desperately searching remedies for the ills that afflict the social order.

Problems

** Everything has not gone well with wealth and affluence attained through phenomenally high rates of growth of GNP. Even some of the most developed among the more developed countries find themselves perenially facing the problems of cycles of economic recession, soaring inflation and growing unemployment. Their inability to resolve intra-society contradictions, disharmony and imbalance is pathetic. Young people are in revolt. Having set their sights on goals beyond material prosperity, they from time to time evolve counter-cultures which are symptomatic of certain forms of sickness that have permeated these societies. The search for alternative lifestyles and different kinds of experience draws them to exotic cults imported from outside or innovated within. The rationality of the system is challenged by women's liberation, which has demonstrated that in the present social order woman is only seen as a part-person, if not a non-person, and is used symbolically as a sex object. Pockets of endemic poverty persist even in the most developed societies. Violence continues to increase and the erosion of moral values no longer causes revulsion. Corruption has become a way of life and is being rationalized. If these are necessary and inevitable aspects of modernization, the Third World would rather avoid it; but this is easier said than done. What happens in affluent countries acquires a powerful hold over the less developed countries. The lifestyles of the former are often initiated uncritically. This change does not accord with the norms and traditions of society, which is pulled in contrary directions. This explains why there are breakdowns of modernization, why tradition reasserts itself and why even extreme forms of fundamentalism attract eager and dedicated adherents. The many accomplishments of modernization are astonishing; but its failures in human engineering are puzzling. Lopsided growth creates as many problems as it solves.

Consider in this context the misdirection of science and technology that are causing global discord and disharmony. Money can readily be found to create new tools of destruction; but the affluent countries cannot put aside even 1% or 2% of their GNP for the development of the Third World. Military assistance is more easily given than development assistance. Think of what the cost of a sophisticated F-16 bomber, atomic submarine or ground-to-air or air-to-air missile system could buy in terms of food, health and education. Hunger need not be a problem for there is enough food to go round. The trap lies in the inability of a large majority to afford it. The future can be different, as the emerging discipline of biotechnology holds out the prospect of providing limitless supplies of food and fuel through the production of protein from hydrocarbon and fuel from plant waste and algae. This new technology, with immense possibilities, is still in an experimental stage. It remains to be seen if resources for its full development can be made available to free millions of the world's poor from their precarious subsistence living and solve the global energy crisis.

Nor need disease be a problem. Modern medicine has treatment for most, if not all, human ailments. The only snag is that multi-nationals have artificially pegged the prices so that even some common treatments are beyond the reach of the poor. Further inputs into medical research can find cheap and effective remedies for the common ailments that afflict, debilitate and subsequently kill the poor prematurely. Even the more deadly killers are not intractable. It is a question of getting priorities right and transferring even a small portion of global financial resources towards strengthening these strategies of survival. As of now the cynical international order appears more interested in costly war games than in solving survival problems.

All projections towards AD 2000 are cheerless and point to the likelihood of the widening of the gap between the rich and the poor. In 1975 the world population was estimated to be 4,090 million; in the year 2000 it is likely to have grown to 6,351 million. In the more developed countries it will rise from 1,131 million in 1975 to 1,323 million in 2000; in the less developed countries, from 2,959 in 1975 to 5,028 million in 2000. The world's population will have increased by 55% by 2000. Of this, 17% will be in the more developed regions and 70% in the less developed. Thus, by the year 2000, the more developed regions will have 21% and the less developed regions 79% of human population. By regions, Africa will have 13%, Asia and the Pacific 57%, Latin America 10%, the USSR and Eastern Europe 7% and North America, Western Europe, Japan, Australia and New Zealand 13%. Thus, roughly 20% will belong to the developed regions and 80% to the less developed. Contrast this with projected GNP estimates for the year 2000. The GNP of the entire world is estimated by then to be 14,677 billion of constant 1975 dollars; of this $11,224 billion will be in more developed regions and only $3,452 billion in the less developed regions. The Gross National Product of the United States, again in billions of constant 1975 dollars, is likely to be $3,530 billion and of Western Europe $3,740 billion as against the $718 billion of the Peoples' Republic of China, $198 billion of India, and only $21 billion of Pakistan and $19 billion of Bangladesh. These randomly chosen projections are presented here only to indicate the nature of the widening gap.

The situation can be best summarized by quoting from the major findings of the *Global 2000 Report: Entering the Twenty-First Century* (1981).[6]

Rapid growth in world population will hardly have altered by 2000. The world's population will grow from 4 billion in 1975 to 6.35 billion in 2000, an increase of more than 50 per cent. The rate of growth will slow only marginally, from 1.8 per cent a year to 1.7 per cent. In terms of sheer numbers, population will be growing faster in 2000 than it is today, with 100 million people added each year compared with 75 million in 1975. Ninety per cent of this growth will occur in the poorest countries.

While the economies of the less developed countries (LDCs) are expected to grow at faster rates than those of the industrialized nations, the gross national product per capita in most LDCs remains low. The average gross national product per capita is projected to rise substantially in some LDCs (especially in Latin America), but in the great populous nations of South Asia it remains below $2,000 a year (in 1975 dollars). The large existing gap between the rich and poor nations widens.

World food production is projected to increase 90 per cent over the 30 years from 1970 to 2000. This translates into a global per capita increase of less than 15 per cent over the same period. The bulk of that increase goes to countries that already have relatively high per capita food consumption. Meanwhile per capita consumption in South Asia, the Middle East and the LDCs of Africa will scarcely improve or will actually decline below present inadequate levels. At the same time, real prices for food are expected to double. Arable land will increase only 4 per cent by 2000, so that most of the increased output of food will have to come from higher yields. Most of the elements that now contribute to higher yields – fertilizer, pesticides, power for irrigation, and fuel for machinery – depend heavily on oil and gas. During the 1980s world oil production will approach geological estimates of maximum production capacity, even with rapidly increasing petroleum prices. The Study projects that the richer industrialized nations will be able to command enough oil and other commercial energy supplies to meet rising demands through 1990. With the expected price increases, many less developed countries will have increasing difficulties meeting energy needs. For the one-quarter of humankind that depends primarily on wood for fuel, the outlook is bleak. Needs for fuelwood will exceed available supplies by about 25 per cent before the turn of the century.

While the world's finite fuel resources – coal, oil, gas, oil shale, tar sands and uranium – are theoretically sufficient for centuries, they are not evenly distributed; they pose difficult economic and environmental problems; and they vary greatly in their amenability to exploitation and use.

Nonfuel mineral resources generally appear sufficient to meet projected demands through 2000, but further discoveries and investments will be needed to maintain reserves. In addition, production costs will increase with energy prices and may make some nonfuel mineral resources uneconomic. The quarter of the world's population that inhabits industrial countries will continue to absorb three-fourths of the world's mineral production.

Regional water shortages will become more severe. In the 1970–2000 period population growth alone will cause requirements for water to double in nearly half the world. Still greater increases would be needed to improve standards of living. In many LDCs, water supplies will become increasingly erratic by 2000 as a result of extensive deforestation. Development of new water supplies will become more costly virtually everywhere.

Significant losses of world forests will continue over the next 20 years as demand for forest products and fuelwood increases. Growing stocks of commercial-size timber are projected to decline 50 per cent per capita. The world's forests are now disappearing at the rate of 18–20 million hectares a year (an area half the size of California), with most of the loss occurring in the humid tropical forests of Africa, Asia and South America. The projections indicate that by 2000 some 40 per cent of the remaining forest cover in LDCs will be gone.

Serious deterioration of agricultural soils will occur worldwide, due to erosion, loss of organic matter, desertification, salinization, alkalinization and waterlogging. Already, an area of cropland and grassland approximately the size of Maine is becoming barren wasteland each year, and the spread of desert-like conditions is likely to accelerate. Atmospheric concentrations of carbon dioxide and ozone-depleting chemicals are expected to increase at rates that could alter the world's climate and upper atmosphere significantly by 2050. Acid rain from increased combustion of fossil fuels (especially coal) threatens damage to lakes, soils, and crops. Radioactive and other hazardous materials present health and safety problems in increasing numbers of countries.

Extinctions of plant and animal species will increase dramatically. Hundreds of thousands of species – perhaps as many as 20 per cent of all species on earth – will be irretrievably lost as their habitats vanish, especially in tropical forests.

What the report has to say in the opening paragraphs of its "Major Findings and Conclusions" is a pointer to the future.

If present trends continue, the world in 2000 will be more crowded, more polluted, less stable ecologically, and more vulnerable to disruption than the world we live in now. Serious stresses involving population, resources, and environment are clearly visible ahead. Despite greater material output, the world's people will be poorer in many ways than they are today.

For hundreds of millions of the desperately poor, the outlook for food and other necessities of life will be no better. For many it will be worse. Barring revolutionary advances in technology, life for most people on earth will be more precarious in 2000 than it is now – unless the nations of the world act decisively to alter current trends.

The most significant question is, *Will nations of the world act decisively to alter the current trend?* This is a challenge to the much proclaimed creative rationality of humanity.

Notes

1. O'Connell, James, "The Concept of Modernization", in Cyril E. Black (ed.), *Comparative Modernization*, New York, The Free Press, 1976.
2. Huntington, Samuel P. "The Change to Change: Modernization, Development, and Politics", in Cyril E. Black (ed.), *Comparative Modernization*, *ibid.*
3. Toffler, Alvin, *The Third Wave*, New York, Bantam Books, 1980.
4. Huntington, "The Change to Change", pp. 155, 174.
5. Toffler, *The Third Wave*.
6. *The Global 2000 Report to the President: Entering the Twenty-first Century*, vol. I, a report prepared by the Council on Environmental Quality and the Department of State, Washington, DC, 1981.

2 Modernization Reconsidered

Birth of a Paradigm

The concept of modernization is the response of Western social science to the many challenges faced by the Third World in the decades immediately following the Second World War. During this period the process of political decolonization had started and empires were breaking up one by one. New nations were entering the community of sovereign states with dramatic rapidity; the political map of the world was changing so fast that cartographers were finding it hard to cope. The Western world had to recognize the emerging reality and work out new modes of co-existence with the former colonies and dependencies. New intellectual relationships were also needed.

The new nations were in a hurry to launch massive programmes of economic development and technical change. The more advanced nations, some of whom were the erstwhile rulers of these territories, decided to extend their cooperation in a limited way to these endeavours. In doing so they were impelled only partly by conscience and humanitarian impulses; strategic power interests and possible long-term economic gain also entered their calculations and influenced their decisions. In the process, they were anxious to evolve stable patterns of relationship that were mutually beneficial; considerations of short- and long-term national interest weighed as much with the developed countries as with the developing ones. Western social science geared itself to aid and assist the international effort at cooperation in change. Funds flowed freely to support research in this direction. The researchers recognized the need to come out with formulations that would not offend the sensitivities of the emerging nations and would offer them, at the same time, attractive paradigms to shape and order their development programmes. Modernization was one such formulation. It held out a model of considerable promise, which held sway for over a decade and a half.

Late in the 1950s some early and tentative versions of this concept began sporadically to appear. The effort was intensified in the first half of the 1960s and by the mid-1960s a powerful interdisciplinary school had grown round the concept. By the end of the decade, however, it had spent much of its force and was losing ground. In the early years of the 1970s the inadequacies of the concept emerged in clear relief and social scientists started looking for alternative paradigms.

There was a certain hypnotic quality about the concept of modernization which attracted a sizable following. An accurate anticipation of the aspirations and urges of the people in the Third World was implicit in it. During the colonial phase, and earlier, poverty, ignorance and disease were accepted and tolerated as necessary evils, for there was little that could be done to eradicate them. With freedom won, governments of the Third World assumed the responsibility of removing poverty and all its attendant evils. Attaining Western levels of affluence may have been a distant goal; but it none the less remained an ideal. Kwame Nkrumah said "We in Ghana will do in ten years what took others one hundred years to do." Nehru echoed these sentiments.

Later it was realized that the attainment of this long-term goal would take time, but some mid-term objectives – assuring larger incomes and better social services – were visualized as achievable targets within stipulated periods of time. The modernization paradigm promised that this could be done. The Third World believed that modernization was necessary, desirable and possible; the idea won eager and enthusiastic acceptance. Those offering development aid promoted this hope in subtle ways.

Another attractive feature of the concept was that it showed an apparent concern for the cultural sensitivities of both the elites and the masses of the Third World. The term "modernization" was much less value-loaded than its predecessor – Westernization. Most countries in the Third World were proud of their cultural heritage and deeply attached to it. While desiring Western standards of plenty they had no desire to abandon their own lifestyles and values. The concept of modernization recognized the strength of roots; it did not pose any overt threat to the cultural identity of the people aspiring for rapid change. To the elite of the Third World the ideal of Westernization was difficult to swallow; they accepted modernization readily because it did not appear to offend their cultural dignity. The change of terminology, however, did not change the objective and motivation of modernization, which assiduously worked to Westernize "backward cultures" of developing societies.

The academic respectability of the concept also contributed to its easy acceptability. In the mid-1960s it was a synthesis of the insights and intellectual resources of several social science disciplines – history, political science, sociology, psychology and economics. Each discipline made an individual contribution, but the concept itself was an amalgam. Some established and emerging reputations were associated with the concept. Third World scholarship, not as yet completely decolonized, unsuspectingly grabbed it.

The flow and promise of international aid had created an atmosphere favourable to Western ideas and ideals of development. Some aid was received, more was expected. This also contributed to the enthusiastic and somewhat uncritical welcome accorded to the modernization approach. The far reaching implications of foreign aid were only critically appraised and understood later.

Modernization: Attributes and Indicators

Modernity may be understood as the common behavioural sssystem historically associated with the urban, industrial, literate and participant societies of Western Europe and North America. This system is characterized by a rational and scientific world view, growth and the ever increasing application of science and technology, together with the continuous adaptation of the institutions of society to the imperatives of the new world view and the emerging technological ethos. These societies have registered impressive economic growth and continue to do so. It will be recalled that the most dramatic changes took place during the middle and closing decades of the 19th Century, although the origins of the modernization can be traced back to fifteenth- and sixteenth-century Europe. Early in the twentieth century Japan, the first Asian country to do so, joined the race for industrialization. Later, the USSR as well as some other countries, achieved modernization in varying degrees. Many other aspirants have also succeeded, at least partially, in acquiring different levels of modernization; some of them are pushing forward for more of it.

Three assumptions are basic to the concept of modernization:

1. Inanimate sources of power must be increasingly tapped with a view to solving human problems and ensuring minimum acceptable standards of living, the ceiling of which should rise progressively.

2. Towards this end there should be both individual and collective effort. The collective dimension is important because associational capability to operate complex organizations is a prerequisite of at least the middle and higher reaches of modernization.

3. To create and run complex organizations radical personality change and attendant changes in the social structure and values are necessary.

Thus, the complex processes of modernization assume a series of interpenetrating and interdependent transformations. On the level of personality, it is now widely recognized, they envisage promotion of rationality as well as empathy, mobility and high participation. (The technical sense in which these terms are used will be discussed later.) These attributes of a "modernized" personality are promoted and sustained by structural, institutional, attitudinal and value change on the personal, social, and cultural levels. In sociological language, the social and cultural milieu increasingly acquires achievemental, universalistic and specificity-oriented emphases. Modernized societies accept and produce more innovations, build up associational capability and sharpen problem-solving abilities. The absence of fit between the modernized personality and the social/cultural framework may lead to an uncomfortable imbalance. For this reason, harmonizing and interlinking changes in the personality, cultural and social systems is essential. In the context of modernization these transformations should be viewed as a precondition to the growth of complex organizations that effectively exploit energy from inanimate sources for human well-being and prosperity.

The most essential attribute of modernization according to the paradigm, is *rationality*, a term that recurs frequently in the treatment of the theme, but has nowhere been defined with acceptable precision. Rationality transforms thought processes at the level of the individual and in the process permeates the entire institutional framework of society. Events and situations are understood in terms of cause and effect and strategies of action are determined by careful ends–means calculations. The traditional world view understands and explains worldly phenomena in an other worldly idiom; modernization substitutes a scientific world view. In consequence, mythical and supernatural explanations are consistently ignored so that a point is reached when, for major areas of human activity, they become nonfunctional. This transformation does not remain confined only to individual thought processes; it is reflected also in the working of the institutions that set the goals of society and determine instrumentalities for their realization. Rationality begins to characterize all forms of human interaction and enters into people's vision of a new future as well as into their strivings for the attainment of the objectives they set themselves. The concomitant structural changes and value shifts bring about fundamental changes in the entire cultural ethos.

As a result of serious interdisciplinary endeavours focused on modernization, an impressive inventory of its attributes has been prepared. It covers individuals, their attitudes and values. It also extends to the value framework of society and its components. It envisions a new future for society and contemplates investing new functions in old institutions and building new institutions to serve the reformulated goals of society through redefined institutional means.

According to Lerner (1958) three features constitute the core of modernized personality – empathy, mobility, and high participation.[1] Individuals react to events and situations according to their perceptions of the social scene. A modernized individual, endowed with empathy, will also take note of how events and situations are perceived by others. Empathy, in other words, is the capacity to see things as others see them. All societies possess this capacity in some measure, but to sharpen and strengthen it can make a qualitative change in human interaction. Such a change is desired in modernized societies.

The second attribute – mobility – does not refer only to geographical mobility – it is used in a more comprehensive sense. The modern world is characterized by constant and rapid change; in it an individual does not remain attached permanently to one primary status and its attendant roles, for which she or he is initially socialized. The imperatives of change demand a capacity to assume, as occasions demand, new statuses and learn to play associated roles. This capacity for status and role switch assumes psychic mobility. Unlike the traditional society, which had ascribed statuses and roles, the modernized society has an open status system. To adapt to it a person has to have a capacity of being able to move from one status to another and assume the associated roles with ease. Without the emergence of mobile personalities the process of modernization is impeded.

In the traditional order a person invariably has to accept the social goals, the instrumentalities for their realization and a predetermined role in relation to them. Social objectives are not open to question, the instrumentalities cannot be altered easily and a person cannot normally transcend the grooves set by tradition. The individual, thus, remains passive in respect of the social goals and the ways to achieve them. This changes radically in a modernized society. The compliant individual becomes active and participant, sharing social concerns and freely articulating views about them. A person holds and forms opinions, claims a share in the decision-making processes and is actively involved in action aimed at securing results that reflect self-valuations and judgements. A high degree of participation is expected of an individual in a modernized society.

A personality characterized by empathy, mobility and high participation is further fortified with a complex of desired attitudes and values. The most important of these is achievement motivation – the need to achieve, irrespective of the rewards associated with what is achieved (McClelland, 1976).[2] Striving to get desired results has also to be built into the personalities of individuals (Cantril, 1965).[3] These may not be viewed initially as universal attributes of all citizens, but a crucial minority at least must possess them. As the society modernizes, this minority will increase. Equally important is the presence of faith in both the desirability and possibility of change. A degree of dissatisfaction with the prevailing situation is necessary: it should be reinforced with a strong belief in the capacity of human intervention to make changes in the desired direction. Thus, the inadequacies of the traditional or quasi-traditional orders must be recognized, vision of a new order projected, and faith in human capability to intervene and bring about the contemplated changes strengthened. Until this happens the great push that is needed to move decisively in the direction of modernization will not be forthcoming. Also, inculcation of new attitudes to wealth, work, savings and risk taking is necessary. The objectives of modernization must relate directly to individuals and their families, to their well-being and prosperity. They should be able to visualize, in concrete terms, that working for increasing the national wealth also brings some tangible rewards for themselves and those close to them. Such a realization generates new attitudes to work and imparts a sense of dedication and discipline. With the understanding of the instrumental worth of wealth and its relationship to work, well-defined criteria for the uses of wealth should develop. The realization that wealth can produce more wealth will develop a capacity to put off immediate gratification, encourage savings and promote entrepreneurship. In making rational calculations and choices, it will be necessary also to take some deliberate risks for entrepreneurship can never be 100% safe. Equipped with these attitudes and values a society can expect acceleration of the modernization process.

Changes in individual personality and thought processes lead to changes in the social system, its orientations and emphases. These, in turn, facilitate and stimulate further modifications in personality. Following Parsons' well known pattern variables, modernization assumes major shifts in at least three of these. First, status is determined by achievemental rather than by ascriptive criteria. Second, patterns of interaction are governed by universalistic rather than particularistic norms. Universalistic considerations, in other words, provide the normative bases for relationships. Third, expectations and obligations in the system of role relationships acquire greater specificity and replace the diffuse system that characterized the traditional order. The character of a modern society is rational in cognitive aspects, universalistic in membership aspects, functionally specific in substantive definitional aspects, neutral in affective aspects, individualistic in the goal orientation aspect and hierarchical in stratification aspects. Units of society tend to be more specialized and self-sufficient, there is a combination of centralization and decentralization, and a noticeable growth of centralized media of exchange and markets. There is increasing evidence of role differentiation, solidarity and integration. The modern society, according to Eisenstadt (1966), emerges as a consensual mass society and ultimately crystallizes as a nation state.[4]

There are also changes in the political dimension. Modernized societies have greater interest articulation, formation of strong interest groups, and institutionalized political competition. Networks of political communication gradually develop and acquire strength; institution building for participative decision making is emphasized.

Modernized societies operate through institutional structures that are capable of continuously absorbing the changes that are inherent in the process of modernization. The consensual mass society, to which a reference has been made, encompasses a large proportion of the population and assumes its participation in the vital processes of decision-making. A series of complex organizations – specialized and differentiated, relatively self-sufficient and functionally specific – undertake to discharge functions in diverse and disparate fields: production of new knowledge and its application to human situations and problems, adapting old knowledge to new situations and problems, diffusion of knowledge and its applications, planning (including mobilization and allocation of resources) and management of change (including handling of obstacles and breakdowns as well as anticipation of trends and likely problems and formulation of strategies to deal with them), crisis resolution and dealing with anomic disturbances, capital formation and making of critical inputs and so forth. The organizational context of life undergoes parallel significant changes. The roles of family- and kinship-based organizations get more narrowly defined; governments and associated units such as bureaucracy, economic and financial institutions, armed forces and organizations dealing with specific functional areas such as education, health, housing, public transport and recreation, assume increasingly important roles.

The importance of the economic dimension of modernization cannot be minimized. Performance or non-performance in this sphere, in the final analysis, determines the fate of the entire programme of modernization. Economic institutions require support of an adequate administrative and legal framework and an efficient monetary and banking structure. There should be a margin for savings and opportunities for capital formation. The economy should be able to attain a degree of self-sustaining growth sufficient to increase both production and consumption.

This paradigm focuses on certain attributes which are the essential indicators of modernization. On how these and other attributes are to be acquired, the paradigm maintains a tantalizing silence. No step by step strategy has been suggested; no clear cut stages have been postulated. Some significant correlations, however, have been presented. For example, there appears to be a high correlation between the degree of modernization and rates of literacy, levels of exposure to the mass media of communication and extent of urbanization. These are highly suggestive and can indirectly provide guidelines to action.

What has been left unsaid is to be inferred. Education and the media have to be pressed into service to bring about changes in attitudes and values. Structural modifications will perhaps need the pressure of public opinion and purposive state action. Imaginative and systematic efforts will have to be directed towards institution building for accomplishing the highly specialized and differentiated tasks implicit in the process of modernization. The paradigm does not go beyond this; it is not a blueprint for action.

Barriers and Breakdowns

It was not difficult to foresee and identify likely obstacles in the path of modernization even while this concept was in its infancy. Indeed some notes of warning were sounded even at the time it was first offered to the Third World: forces of tradition will not yield without a series of battles; primordial loyalties will assert themselves time and again, making nation building difficult; torn between its allegiance to tradition and commitment to modernization the Third World élite is likely to falter and dilute the vigour of its pursuit; sloppy and inept planning and management of modernization programmes may impede their progress; even the relatively "successful" programmes may encounter unanticipated fundamentalist reactions at the most unexpected turns. Most of these arguments were well taken; but it has to be borne in mind that all the anticipated barriers and the possible causes of breakdowns of modernization were seen as lying essentially within the societies that were aspiring to modernize themselves. External factors and forces obstructing the modernization process were not brought into consideration.

Subsequent experience was to confirm some of the earlier forebodings. The gap between the promise and performance of modernization was too wide to escape notice. The projected pay-off was nowhere in sight, prosperity was continuing to elude the Third World. The revolution of rising expectations was in danger of turning into an encounter with mounting frustrations. Absence of results generated mass apathy and anger and left the modernizing élite confused. What went wrong? And where? Why were things not going the expected way? Barriers to modernization, so far a theme mostly of academic interest, now became a serious diagnostic concern. And this happened at a time when theoretic refinements were still being worked into the concept of modernization.

It was observed that programmes of modernization mainly attempted to transfer technology, without effecting necessary institutional changes. The need for the latter was recognized, but for a variety of reasons programmes in this field had either to be put off or were accorded low priority. In other words, the attempt was made to gear the traditional framework of society to the tasks of attaining the goals of modernization. But modernization, as C.E. Black (1966) perceptively puts it, is

> the process by which historically evolved institutions are adapted to the rapidly changing functions that reflect the unprecedented increase in man's knowledge, permitting control over his environment, that accompanied the scientific revolution.[5]

The adaptive processes were left free, by and large, to shape themselves. They were not being guided or directed, for not much was known about effective ways of doing so. In fact many of these societies even lacked the necessary infrastructure – education was backward, modern mass media were poorly developed; transport facilities were primitive; public health standards were appallingly low; and formal organizations with trained personnel to take up the complex tasks of development existed only in an embryonic form. The complexities of the process of development were not sufficiently understood; their covert and ramifying dimensions, especially, remained an uncharted territory. As such, both the leadership and the developmental bureaucracy were unprepared to meet setbacks and breakdowns. They found it hard to fulfil their eloquently made promises.

Gaining wisdom from hindsight an attempt was made to locate and understand the barriers to modernization. Analyses of the ideological, motivational, institutional and organizational inadequacies of the developing societies were undertaken as a diagnostic exercise. They were expected to suggest some correctives also.

Ideological Barriers

The anti-colonial and anti-imperialist struggles had developed a sense of nationalism in most of the Third World countries, but few of them had attained true and full national integration. The nationalistic stand against foreign domination had temporarily masked many divisive tendencies within; with the attainment of independence sub-nationalisms of various kinds – ethnic, linguistic, regional and religious – began to assert themselves. The fragile texture of the national bond resulted in diluting the emerging nationalism and this, in turn, weakened the ideological motivation for development.

Most developing societies launched their programmes of modernization with blurred images and conflicting goals. In some societies there was a strong urge to revert to an idealized past; in others attempts were made to revitalize some aspects of tradition. While the tractor was desired, the ox plough was unfailingly idealized. The modern ideals of democracy, secularism, and socialism, were projected; but at the same time both the élite and the masses continued to refer back to some Golden Age in the past. The pulls of the past and of the desired future, in many situations, were equally strong. The result was ambiguity, confusion and contradiction in the formulation of the goals of change. Such formulations were often an uneasy and untenable compromise between tradition and modernity.

The aims of modernization – watered down as they were – often did not percolate down to the masses. This could be attributed to inadequate and imperfect communication between the élite and the masses. Channels of communication were poorly developed and the presentation of the development message was rarely effective. As a result, there was little consonance between the modernization objectives as formulated by the élite and their acceptance by the masses. Indifferent and weak communication thus contributed to low ideological articulation.

In this context we should also examine the congruence or otherwise in the ultimate and proximate goals of modernization. The former represented a lofty formulation; but in determining the proximate objectives – targets for the immediate future – uneasy pragmatic adjustments and self-defeating situational compromises had to be made. The outcome, occasionally at least, appeared to be pulling away from the modernization objective.

Finally, we have to consider the dramatic contrast between the profession and the practice of the élite and leadership. In many countries they entrenched themselves in positions of power and surrounded themselves with privileges. They were unwilling to surrender the advantages of tradition and tried to corner for themselves all the benefits of modernization. This often led to the puzzlement of the poor who did not know what to believe and what not to believe. This naturally resulted in a loss of credibility for the ideology of modernization. It may be noted that the élite, its radical rhetoric and populist postures notwithstanding, dragged its feet when it came to implementing structural changes.

Motivational Barriers

Barriers on the motivational level were also many and complex. They were mostly the products of poor ideological articulation. The masses in the

Third World generally had constricted mental horizons and low achievement motivation. The belief that society could and should be transformed, and that change was desirable and necessary, had not taken roots in their minds. The urge to participate in the adventure of modernization was not widely diffused. In point of fact, the poor had no voice in determining the contents of schemes intended to benefit them: they were dumb witnesses to the drama that was being staged in their name. Development projects were launched with great fanfares, but there was no strategy on offer to sustain the effort; few projects showed the desired results.

Lack of social discipline was yet another impediment to the successful implementation of programmes of modernization. Broad national objectives and narrow sectional interests were frequently in conflict: the means adopted for the attainment of the latter increasingly bordered on deviance. In the absence of strong social sanctions and effective enforcement, which could hold them in check, anomic and parochial tendencies gained strength. Scarce national resources were destroyed with impunity, the administration looked on helplessly finding itself unable to intervene. This trend partially undid parts of the small gains registered by national efforts to ensure economic development.

Torn between national and parochial pulls, and between short-run and long-term interests, the masses tended to oscillate between the two. A determined modernization effort was never mounted. Even in those exceptional cases where it was generated, motivation could not be sustained.

Institutional Barriers
It has been argued that the institutional framework of Third World societies – characterized by ascription, particularism, affectivity, and diffused expectations – was not particularly propitious for modernization. In retrospect, it is amazing how little effort was made to bring about structural modification and institutional change; the efforts that were made were feeble and faltering. The vested interests of different sections of the modernizing élite effectively blocked some alterations. The precarious security available in the culture of poverty amazingly worked against structural and institutional change aimed at its eradication. Sacred emphases in the thought processes and working habits of the masses did not permit the emergence of new attitudes characterized by "rationality". For want of a functional analogue ritual continued to maintain its predominant position. Finally, there were pronounced incongruities between the political/administrative systems and the social system – and yet also an amazing alliance among them. Consider, in this context, the marriage of caste to democracy in India. In some significant ways the two are antithetical to each other and yet in the Indian polity they appear to have forged supportive links.

Organizational Barriers
In most Third World countries the local and national political processes at best were loosely integrated; the links between micro- and macro-political

processes were tenuous. Half-hearted, and often unimaginative, efforts to bring about integration between them did not register any conspicuous gains.

The reach of administration was limited and it was hamstrung by a variety of factors. The pressures of the system were too strong on it to permit the public services to approximate to the Weberian ideal-type attributes. The demands of the system and the erratic and unreasonable dictates of the new political élite made it difficult for it to function on rational principles. Besides, the personnel lacked the training, experience and expertise demanded of them by the ideology and programme of modernization. Added to this, the legitimacy of the government itself was yet to be firmly established.

Institutional paucity and poverty were in evidence in almost all functional areas impinging on modernization. Either the required institutions did not exist or they were afflicted with serious maladies which impaired their functioning. Planning and communication were considered key areas; both had significant inadequacies. Planning techniques used were imitative and inept. The development programme itself lacked a sense of priorities. This is explained, at least partially, by the failure of these countries to evolve effective planning machinery and strategy. The development of communication – political and developmental – left much to be desired, because an adequate institutional infrastructure had not been created for it. Production of new knowledge and technology, including adaptation of technology, left much to be desired. The situation was similar for many other strategic areas and vital tasks. Creation of an adequate institutional base was an urgent desideratum; but the leadership did not know how to go about it with the required imagination and political will.

These factors, among others, explained the halting and hesitating progress of modernization in developing societies. Though the broad symptoms were recognized, attempts at accurate and penetrating diagnoses were few. The therapeutic aspect continued to bristle with doubts and uncertainties, posing a series of continuing challenges to the modernizing élite.

Decline of the Paradigm

The modernization approach had a brief but illustrious career: it dominated the social science scene in the West and in several parts of the Third World for a decade. Between the late 1950s and the mid-1960s it reached its peak. Towards the end of the 1960s it began to lose its appeal. Faced with mounting multidisciplinary criticism, it found it hard to maintain its preeminent position. By the mid-1970s the entire gamut of theories revolving round the question of a desired, preferred and possible future for the Third World had undergone rigorous and penetrating examination, which brought out into the open their many inadequacies. In the process, the concept of modernization was demystified. By the end of the 1970s it was still lingering on, less on account of its analytic rigour and prognostic potential, more as a matter of habit. But its days were numbered.

In retrospect, the formulation served a useful, though limited, purpose. Perhaps the most productive spin-off from the prodigious scholarly endeavour it generated was the identification of personality attributes, value orientations and societal characteristics associated with the achievement of phenomenal economic progress and social transformation by the application of science and technology, first in Western Europe and North America and later in some other countries that entered the arena of modernity. The inventory of personality and societal attributes was indeed useful and the case for most of the entries in it was more or less convincingly argued. There is little doubt that each of these attributes figured, in a significant measure, in the process of modernization. The inventory was by no means comprehensive. None the less it did identify a number of significant characteristics that could make a critical difference to the direction, rate and quality of progress and goal-oriented change. These characteristics make some adaptive demands on societies seeking to modernize themselves; the outcome depends measurably on the response of the societies to these demands.

This positive aspect notwithstanding, the modernization framework was not without theoretical ambiguities and inadequacies. The notion of rationality, the cornerstone of modernization paradigm, was ambiguous. It is now recognized that rationality can be of different kinds at different levels and in different contexts. The explanatory power of the paradigm was limited and the guidelines to action embodied in it were somewhat obscure. It was evasive on the vital issue of the poverty of the masses, especially in the less developed countries. Two basic questions remained unanswered: *Whose modernization? Modernization for what?* The formulation did not adequately take into account the qualitative changes in the problems that humanity faces, nor did it explore the prospects of modernization and development against the backdrop of the realities of the contemporary world order. The exploitative and repressive aspects of the contemporary world order were not seriously questioned and the alternative of a revolution was ruled out. Thus, the global context of modernity, remained unexamined. Many vital questions regarding the desirability and possibility of modernization are left unasked. This bars the search for meaningful alternatives and inhibits reflection and action aimed at appropriate therapy.

Ambiguities and Inadequacies

The different categories of attributes and indicators of modernization stand out as a positive and generally acceptable contribution; their correlation with varying degrees and levels of modernization has been satisfactorily established. This should not lead us, however, to confuse the effect with the cause. That the constellation of personality, value and societal traits and orientations that sustained the modernization process were themselves the products of a conjunction of socio-economic forces, which provided the initial impetus, can also be argued convincingly. The two – the attributes and the process – mutually reinforce and support each other. The process undeniably plays a role in creating the desired attitudes. Scholars have found a positive correlation between modernization on the one hand and urbanization, literacy rates and media exposure on the other.

There is considerable ambiguity in regard to the human dimension of modernization. Who is to be brought under its umbrella? The intention may be to benefit all sections of the population in modernizing societies, but nowhere has this been stated explicitly. The special needs of the weak and the vulnerable, in the context of the modernization process, are not specifically mentioned. Similarly, the object of modernization has not been spelled out in distributive terms, nor has it been related to the wider question of the quality of life. Equality and social justice have not figured prominently in the discussion. Like dominant Western development theory, the modernization formulation also fails to pose some significant questions. The assumption under the former was that higher GNP, leading to higher national income, would enrich a nation as a whole; modernization makes the same fallacious assumption and addresses its programmes to the amorphous mass of society rather than to particular, especially the needy, sections of it. It is not realized that under certain conditions the magic of the market place simply does not work. The trickle down effect is weak and the invisible hand often misses the poor and the vulnerable.

Modernization lays emphasis on the ever increasing use of science and technology through complex organizations. The more advantaged sections of society have easier access to both and are in a position to manipulate the organizations in such a way that the maximum benefits accrue to them. The less advantaged are likely to suffer continued neglect. It is in fact possible and is convincingly shown in some well documented cases – that in the midst of general growth the poor actually register a lowering of their standards of living.

As no social indicators are built into the modernization formulation its social objectives are neither specific nor quantifiable. The dimension remains blurred, though it is possible to draw some inferences about it from the inventory of indicators of modernization. It should be noted that the objectives of modernization have not been related to the paramount consideration of social justice. What is most lacking is the projection of an integral vision incorporating imaginative plans for enriching the quality of life – from meeting minimum needs to the promotion of higher creativity. Nothing better than the lacklustre Western style of development is promised. The considerable achievements of Western type of modernization need not be deprecated; but at the same time note should be taken of its inner crises and of the threat it poses to genuine global development. The Third World, as an alternative, can de-emphasize personal consumption and concentrate on providing better community services.

The modernization approach, as mentioned earlier, has limited explanatory power and it tends to gloss over some of the uglier aspects of the development process in the West. The West was able to modernize itself, it would appear to say, because its citizens had all the desirable personality attributes and value orientations. Colonial possessions, with access to cheap raw materials and labour as well as a captive market, also contributed significantly to the rapid industrialization of the West. This forced and unequal partnership of the colonies and dependencies in the economic growth of the West remains unacknowledged by modernization theorists. The retardation of the less developed countries, again, is explained in terms of their tradition that is believed to obstruct modernization. Here again the corrosive and debilitating role of colonialism is glossed over. The prevalence of various forms of neocolonialism is not even hinted at. The more positive aspects of tradition do not get a balanced assessment and their potential to inspire modernization remains unexamined.

The suggestions for action offered by the concept are woolly and misleading. Structural change is mentioned; but no directions for it are set and no viable strategies suggested. Because of insufficient understanding of the character of the modernizing élite in these countries, they are assigned certain roles which ultimately go against their interests. Nor is it easy, or perhaps necessary, to demolish tradition. It survives not because the people in the less developed countries love social and cultural antiquities, but the functions performed by its different elements – from customs to institutions – render its continuation both necessary and desirable. Unless a functional analogue, more compatible with the demands of modernization, is found to replace it, the destruction of tradition is likely to create a vacuum. The economic base and the associated social milieu that sustains tradition needs to be changed first; the process will not work in the reverse. Education and communication can bring about limited attitudinal change; but it is not likely that this will lead directly to the major structural transformations that are really called for. The real, and hard but viable, options have not been suggested. Experience shows that tinkering with the symptoms rarely produces the desired structural alterations.

The framework of modernization, as it was presented to us, failed to allow for the problems it was likely to generate. Modernization places great reliance on science and technology. It is assumed that most human problems can be solved by injecting increasingly larger doses of them and by ceaselessly working for their greater sophistication. Some consequences of this trend of thought are bound to prove counter-productive. Much advanced technology is capital-intensive. As it becomes more sophisticated, it requires a relatively small but highly skilled labour force. In the less developed countries capital is scarce and competing claims on it are many. The labour force is large, but its highly skilled component is infinitesimal. Employment generation for the many is a major problem for these countries. At the same time demands of efficiency and economy make the utilization of high technology imperative, at least in some sectors. Developmental aid often comes with strings attached and, as we shall see shortly, deft fingers manipulate the strings in such a way that the technology of the less developed countries emerges as a satellite of the dominant technology of the developed nations. This increases and even perpetuates national inequalities. Lopsided development results when high cost sophisticated technology is introduced in a few sectors, to the neglect of others. Most developing countries, in addition, have a problem of growing unemployment. The choice of advanced technology, in the initial phase at least, can aggravate it. These contradictions have to be resolved and technological options have to be picked with great care. Low capital and labour-intensive technology provides one answer. Appropriate technology, tailored to the needs of these countries, also has to be developed systematically. This is necessary, but not enough. In many critical areas, in defence for example, there are internal pressures and external encouragement to adopt the latest technology. In many instances this proves to be a costly fallacy. Liberation struggles of former colonies were not won by such technology. Vietnam faced the defeated modern technology by sheer determination and adaptable, guerrilla tactics. We also have to consider the problems and consequences of global imbalances if a pronounced technological gap is allowed to persist between the developed and the less developed countries. The latter must never yield to pressures that permanently condemn them to a low technology status.

The projected path of modernization is tied up with technologies that consume a great deal of energy, mostly from non-renewable sources. Because of the current energy crisis even the developed one-third of the world is jittery; the development plans of the less favourably placed two-thirds are in a total disarray. Modern science undoubtedly has the capability to develop alternative sources of energy; but this would require substantial inputs into research and development. Wide and effective diffusion of the results will take its own time, there is a point beyond which it cannot be accelerated. Adaptation costs will also be considerable. These constraints will work to the detriment of the less developed countries.

The relationship between energy from such sources as fossil fuels and electricity and modernization can be overstated. The per capita consumption of energy and a country's standard of living are related in complex ways; but increased availability and utilization of energy do not necessarily raise the standards of living and improve the quality of life of large sections of the population. Energy production and utilization statistics can be highly deceptive; the realities behind them have to be examined closely.

In this connection we must keep in mind another set of consequences of modernization. The process, for its success, requires a combination of technology, adequate infrastructural support and efficient management. Without these, energy sources cannot be harnessed adequately, and complex organizations set up for the purpose cannot be run effectively. Both lead to the impersonalization of the quality of relationships. Is this a gain or a loss? The gains are all too visible, but the invisible loss also merits consideration. The accent on individual autonomy – a new measure of freedom – leads to the weakening of the collective bond. The trend may produce anomie and alienation. These features are fraught with grave social consequences. The new sense of liberation – freedom from constraints of social mores and religion – adds to the complexity of the situation. A shift from faith to choice is evident, but the choices made can range from the rational to the bizzare. Tradition can be seen to enter surreptitiously into some of these choices. A great many of them, however, are oddities without purpose, of little value other than their novelty. Under conditions of lax discipline the new liberation – freedom of choice – tends to be grossly abused. Purposive social guidance is missing. The directions provided earlier by cultural tradition and religion having become feeble, and other sanctions having been corroded by growing permissiveness, society has to experiment and learn several of its lessons the hard way.

It may be added that most of the rewards and riches of modernization are in the nature of a postdated cheque, to be cashed not now but at some indeterminate date in the future. At any rate this is so for the masses. There is no definite date for their realization. This naturally slackens popular zeal for modernization; people can be persuaded to toil and undergo privations more easily if the prize, or a part of it at least, is within reach in the foreseeable future or at least within their lifetime, and not intended for a vague posterity to which they cannot directly relate. The hungry and the exploited have only a limited stock of patience and the present means to them much more than a remote future of which they will not be a part.

The stress in the modernization approach is on material gains; psychic rewards are not adequately mentioned. Provision of the basic material needs of life is undeniably necessary; but beyond these people also require a margin for comfort and creative pursuits. Equating success with a surfeit of creature comforts, in many developing societies reflects the value system of those who are new to affluence; the valuations of succeeding generations could be different. It is possible that these generations may react adversely to most of the status symbols assiduously acquired by their progenitors and find them a meaningless display of ostentation and even vulgarity. Appropriate psychic rewards, on the other hand, always motivate people, but they have, however, to be devised carefully and invested with acceptable meanings and sanctions. People's other-regarding impulses can be put to productive and creative uses, ensuring the well-being of the many instead of promoting selfish pursuits for the few.

Yet another fallacious assumption is implicit in the modernization approach. The modernizing élite and the early beneficiaries of the modernization process do not necessarily spearhead the diffusion of its gains to the entire society. The Western analogy does not appear to be holding true in the case of many less developed countries. According to the historical experience of the developed countries of the West, urban pressures were instrumental also in raising the living standards of the non-urban population. The experience of the less developed countries, on the contrary, suggests an opposite trend: the privileged urban sector, including its working class organizations, aggressively demonstrate their hostility to all equalizing measures. In this instance history is not repeating itself. The Western experience continues to remain important, but the insights drawn from it should not be applied blindly to the programmes of modernization in the Third World.

* Environmental Constraints

The gospel of ceaseless and limitless modernization has been challenged powerfully from other quarters, especially by environmentalists and conservationists. Their persuasively argued and well documented case compels attention. A few of them may have adopted an extremist posture and may ultimately prove to be alarmists; but the caution that they counsel cannot be merely shrugged off. The more balanced exponents of this new concern articulate some serious misgivings about the direction and desirability of modernization (at any rate of modernization along its chosen path). In this context it may be noted that the modernization debate, while speaking volubly about the necessity of changes in cultural tradition and social structure, has said relatively little about the desirability of the reorientation of science and technology.

The environmentalists appear to suggest that, far from being an unmixed blessing limitless modernization may prove to be the undoing of the human race. The situation can only be saved if a new direction is taken immediately.

* Non-renewable natural resources, on which the edifice of modernization is built, are being rapidly depleted and adequate, efficient and economic substitutes are not yet in sight. The search is on, inspired and supported largely by the warnings of critics from this school. Much of the work, especially in the energy field, is still experimental and has a long way to go before it can offer adequate functional analogues for conventional energy sources. The interregnum, between the depletion of some key resources and their replacement by satisfactory substitutes, holds out the frightening prospect of major economic and social upheavals. Resource exhaustion has not yet occurred; but the world is beginning to have a foretaste of it.

* The consequences of environmental pollution and ecological imbalance may be more lethal. Fumes and effluents from modern industries; indiscriminately used chemical fertilizers, pesticides and weed-killers; thoughtless exploitation of natural resources and injuries inflicted on flora and fauna; and above all the visible and invisible destruction caused by modern wars, are playing havoc with our environment. The earth's surface – land and water – as well as its atmosphere are becoming seriously polluted; in some parts of the world pollution has reached dangerous levels which threaten the survival of all living things. This situation is a product of rash modernization.

The *Limits to Growth* type of logic is an unduly alarmist overreaction. Leontief's *Future of the World Economy* (1977) gives a somewhat more hopeful profile of the year 2000.[6] The situation is not without hope; undeniably correctives can be found. But at the same time the warnings of the environmentalists should not go unheeded.

Attempts at freezing the world at the present levels of development would be a desperate remedy. It would be unfair and, of course, it would not work. It would be unfair because those who are underdeveloped would be advised to reconcile themselves to their backwardness in the name of resource conservation and checking atmospheric pollution as well as ecological imbalances, while the affluent would continue to enjoy at least the present levels of consumption and, at the same time, would continue to deplete natural resources and pollute the environment, perhaps at the present and possibly at a slightly reduced rate. In consequence, for an undoubtedly worthy cause, two-thirds of mankind would be condemned to perpetual poverty. The deprived would revolt against the manifest injustice of the outrageous proposal. The zero-rate-of-growth argument is untenable.

What then? Perhaps a redefinition of modernization is indicated. Consistent with environmental imperatives, it will have to stress the reorientation of science and technology and chart a new course for them. Technology cannot remain sovereign nor can it continue to serve the interests of its present masters. It will have to be harmonized with social needs and regulate its pace and direction to the goals and rate of progress in society. Controlled modernization, tempered with distributive justice, may provide the answer. To raise the standards of the many, it may even be necessary to lower the levels of the privileged few. Unless this is done, humankind cannot be saved from a precipitous fall. An unyielding view of modernization may become the harbinger of the disintegration and ultimate doom of humanity and civilization.

The Global Context

If the environmental constraints severely limit the possibility of modernization and even question its desirability (if its attainment is sought in one particular way), the global context of modernization presents even more awesome prospects.

The contemporary world order is inequitable. This has become a cliché; none the less it conveys a disturbing truth that has significant implications for the future of modernization. Nations of the world have an unequal share of the world's total available resources. The reference here is not to uneven natural endowment between nation and nation, but to the unequal access to and control over known resources. To cite only one glaring example: the United States of America, with only 6% of the world's population consumes over 35% of the world's resources. Other developed countries, similarly, appropriate for themselves sizable chunks of the available resources quite disproportionate to the relative size of their populations. To put it figuratively, the developed one-third corner approximately two-thirds of the world's resources; the less developed two-thirds are left with only one-third of the share for their consumption and development. The inequity of this situation speaks for itself.

The disparities are not confined only to the economic arena; incomparably superior military might gives a tremendous political leverage to the developed countries. The global development scene, in consequence, is characterized by a patron–client relationship. The less developed countries can have only a dependency relationship with their patrons – the developed countries. Aid is nearly always conditional, though the strings are often invisible and harsh terms are invariably disguised. Terms of trade are also weighted in favour of the affluent and the powerful. The patron–client relationship is thus doubly disadvantageous to the less developed countries. Their economies can only develop as essentially satellite economies, complementing the dominant economy to which they are linked. The extent of their growth is naturally circumscribed and can rarely hope to become self-reliant, unless the less developed countries demonstrate their resolve to cut loose from their neocolonial moorings. The affluent and the powerful listen with amused tolerance to the reactive rhetoric of the less developed – the Group of 77 or the nonaligned – may even condescend to enter into an occasional dialogue with them; but they are smug about their own strength. The weak can only bark, not bite. Their latent disunity can always be exploited.

The superordination–subordination nexus, in which the modernization of the less developed countries often takes place, has debilitating consequences for several components of the modernization enterprise. Consider the example of science and technology. The developed countries, when they transfer their technology either for cash or as a part of development aid, generally export obsolete technology which has outlived its utility for them and is to be phased out or scrapped. Environment-polluting technology may also be passed off to the Third World. The less developed countries are encouraged to take up projects that produce materials for industries in the patron country. To support such endeavours the developed countries readily part with the necessary technology. This includes both extractive technology and labour-intensive technology: the first to produce raw and semi-processed materials for the patron country's own industry, the second to spare the patron the prohibitive costs of home labour. The transferred technology often consumes energy at a high rate. Third World scientists, when they are trained in developed countries, are usually trained in fields having a greater relevance for the host countries. Returning home they carry on with the same kind of work, despite its proven irrelevance for national needs. It may sound puzzling, but it is nevertheless true, that Third World scientists have contributed, through their work, more to the enrichment of the developed world than to the development of the less developed. As themes in fashion in high prestige seats of learning abroad enjoy great respectability in Third World universities and research institutions, the trend is not likely to be reversed in the foreseeable future. Science and technology, which are expected to provide continuous impetus and sustenance to modernization, are weighted in favour of the more advantaged nations. In the contemporary world context they do perform these functions; but not as much for the benefit of the less developed countries as for that of the more developed ones.

The technological superiority of the developed nations gives them tremendous advantage over the less developed countries. They have high powered and sophisticated instruments of surveillance giving them access to sensitive information. Knowledge derived from these devices, and other sources, is deftly translated into power. Whichever way we look at the present situation, it is weighted in favour of the more developed countries. This naturally limits the modernizing potential of the less developed countries. It is becoming increasingly evident that for development and modernization of the Third World, reshaping and overhauling of the world order is a precondition. Towards this end there is a global dialogue and debate on alternatives, another kind of development, and a new world order, to replace the discredited paradigm of modernization.

Notes

1. Lerner, Daniel, *The Passing of Traditional Society: Modernizing the Middle East*, Glencoe, Il., The Free Press, 1958.
2. McClelland, David C., *Achieving Society*, New York, Halsted Press, 1976.
3. Cantril, H., *The Pattern of Human Concerns*, New Brunswick, NJ, Rutgers University Press, 1965.
4. Eisenstadt, S.N., *Modernization: Protest and Change*, Englewood Cliffs, NJ, Prentice Hall, 1966.
5. Black, Cyril E., *Dynamics of Modernization*, New York, Harper and Row, 1966.
6. Leontief, Wassily, Ann P. Carter and Peter A. Petri, *Future of the World Economy; a United Nations Study*, New York, Oxford University Press, 1977.

3 Development Reconsidered

The distinction between modernization and development is becoming increasingly blurred: a point has been reached when the two terms can be used interchangeably and almost synonymously. The intellectual history of modernization is rooted in the behavioural sciences; but it does take account of the economic factor as a major variable in the modernizing process. Development, on the other hand, has drawn its main sustenance from economics, although the institutional and motivational dimensions have also explicitly and implicitly figured – and continue to figure – in the discussions on the subject. This is more true of recent developments in the discipline. The growing emphasis in both on the diffusion of their benefits – the distributional dimension – has narrowed the gap further. Today, to a lay – non-specialist – audience the two notions mean one and the same thing; differences between them, if any, have a merely semantic significance. The unflattering experience of the last three decades has sobered the over-enthusiastic exponents of both, who now blush at the untenable claims they made in the past. The two streams, being conscious of the inadequacies and limitations of their analyses, have now turned their attention to the search for alternatives.

There is a hard core left which tenaciously clings to its original orthodoxies, buttressing its position with alibis and rationalizations; but it is no longer a part of the debate's mainstream. It is itself all too conscious of the ground that it has lost: its imperious and magisterial pronouncements have been demystified and do not any longer carry much conviction in the Third World.

New blueprints have entered the debate, some emanating from Third World scholars. Definitive answers are difficult to find on a problem as complex as modernization or development. What augurs well for the possibility of resolving the dilemmas, in intellectual terms, is that the quest has now acquired greater historicity, is based on more solid empirical foundations and no longer fights shy of coming out boldly into the open about some delicate and sensitive issues in respect of which it has so far been the convention either to maintain total silence or make only polite and oblique references. Another healthy trend is the move away from theoretical universalities to cultural and country/regional specificities. Third World scholars have overcome the natural limitations and excesses of the reactive phase and are now in the frontline of the debate; their voices are heard with respect. The climate of international anarchy and general political cynicism notwithstanding, there is convincing evidence that, in some quarters at least, the concern for the survival of humankind, for alternative futures and another kind of development, for an equitable basis of a new world order, is genuine. These are new dimensions added to the debate on development and modernization.

Economic Explanations

The classical view of development, as presented in economics, is relatively simple if not simplistic. Though developmentalism is an old and powerful Western idea, most major Western contributions to development economics, with the exception of Marxism, were made in the 1950s and later. The early thinking adopted the metaphor of growth and it was only at the stage of articulation of protest that the umbilical cord linking development to growth was snapped. For a long time development meant only the capacity of a static and retarded economy to generate and sustain an annual increase in GNP at the rate of 5–7%. W. Arthur Lewis, an eminent exponent of the classical model, was concerned with the growth of output per head of population, not with distribution. He took the latter into account only when wealth accumulated from growth was not ploughed back into production. The growth game – or growthmania – dominated economic thinking for a long time, until its limitations were convincingly demonstrated. Even now it is not quite a spent force.

A brief reference to what is known as the Keynesian model is necessary, not because it is a model in the true sense or because it represents in any way a radical departure from the classical liberal approach, but because Keynes' thinking was particularly influential in the Third World and it inspired the building of several development models. Keynes, it will be recalled, focused his work on determination of aggregate income and employment in advanced capitalist, market economies. His model, developed in the early 1930s, was directed not at explaining development or underdevelopment but at analysing the causes of economic depression and unemployment of the period in the West. According to his model unemployment was caused by insufficient aggregate demand and it could be eliminated by government expenditure to raise the aggregate demand, activate idle or underutilized resources and create jobs. Keynes was dealing with problems of mature capitalism – imperfections of the market as well as over-production and under-consumption. He deviated from the classical liberal line of thinking in only one major respect: he expected the state to intervene in certain situations with a view to discharging its responsibility to maintain stability and ensure the continuous growth of the capitalist system.

Keynesian ideas did exert a considerable indirect influence and the elaboration of Keynes' dynamic theory dominated development thinking for a long time. The celebrated Harrod–Domar model bears the impress of Keynesian economics. The equation, written as $g = s/k$, demonstrates the functional economic relationship in which the growth rate of Gross Domestic Product (g) depends directly on the national savings ratio (s) and inversely on the national capital/output ratio (k). This was an influential explanation of the growth process.

The "big push" theory of Rosenstein-Rodan, emphasizing capital investment as the principal instrument of economic development, also owes its inspiration to Keynes. In brief, it states that to take off into the stage of self-sustaining economic growth the main requirement of less developed countries is massive investment aimed at building the economic infrastructure and promoting rapid industrialization. Hirschman's concept of "unbalanced growth" also belongs to this genre of theories. In all of them a positive role is assigned to the state in the promotion of economic development, at least during the critical transitional stage.

A variation on the classical liberal theme, influenced partly by Keynesian ideas, is Walt W. Rostow's once popular and influential *Stages of Economic Growth* theory of development (1961).[1] Unilinear and evolutionist in conception, this theory posits four well marked stages: (1) the traditional and stagnant low per capita stage; (2) the transitional stage in which preconditions for growth are laid down; (3) the "take-off" stage marking the beginning of the process of economic growth; and (4) the industrialized, mass production and consumption stage, which makes for self-sustaining growth. The secret of development lies in following a set of "tricks" at the traditional and especially at the preconditional stage: the economy must save, not consume, a certain proportion of its national income. Growth involves new investment making net additions to the capital stock. Countries which could save 15–20% of their GNP could develop at a much faster rate than those who saved less. This liberal alternative to Marxism – a non-communist manifesto – assumes that some redistribution is the normal result of growth, although it may not lead to the precise levelling of income per head. The logic is simple: the more the economy produces, the more there will be for everyone to share. For the early stages, however, Rostow recommends that surpluses generated by agriculture should be invested into the industrial sector; later a progressive income tax could be imposed.

This approach, and its various later elaborations and refinements, emphasized capital accumulation, the growth of the labour force and the technological progress as the principal components of economic growth.

The absence of these factors, by implication, could explain the economic backwardness of societies. Four major inadequacies can be identified in it: (1) its explanation of economic development is partial and narrow and says little about the role of colonialism in the early stimulation and development of industrialization in some countries; (2) it does not satisfactorily explain the economic backwardness of many countries, especially in relation to their long encounter with imperialism; (3) it assigns a limited role to the state, and that too under certain stipulated conditions; and (4) it is not sufficiently sensitive to poverty and de-emphasizes distribution. Marxist, neo-Marxist, and other radical critics, have trained their guns on the first two of these inadequacies. Keynes opened the door to limited state action, the area of which was gradually enlarged. The socialist economies, i.e. the Soviet Union and others following its model were, and still are, centrally planned. But the Third World – much of it emerging from erstwhile colonial empires – also took the path of planned development. In respect of the fourth – poverty and redistribution – there was some serious heart searching within the liberal tradition itself.

As is well known, the "vicious circle of poverty" – a self-reinforcing situation under which certain undesirable factors lead from one to the other until the circle is completed, e.g. poverty leads to low consumption, which leads to poor health, which leads to low productivity, which contributes to the persistence of poverty – is an established explanation of economic backwardness. But it is at best a partial explanation and the only remedy it can suggest is essentially the one which the classical liberal model has to offer. Much the same idea has been elaborated by Myrdal (1970) under what he calls the process of "circular cumulative causation", though his treatment is more sophisticated and contains some prescriptions for action.[2] His emphasis is on institutional change. The inter-nation structure approach, to be discussed later, went into the problem in greater depth and explored its historical, sociological and economic dimensions.

In the meantime there were second thoughts on the goals of development. The glitter of growth was fading, the invisible hand (Adam Smith's 1776 argument that unbridled pursuit of individual self-interest automatically leads to the maximization of the social interest) was not working the expected miracles, and distribution was coming to the fore under the new slogan of "redistribution with growth". Dudley Seers (1969) has articulated this concern simply but effectively.[3]

> The questions to ask about a country's development are therefore: What has been happening to poverty? What has been happening to unemployment? What has been happening to inequality? If all three of these have declined from high levels, then beyond doubt this has been a period of development for the country concerned. If one or two of these central problems have been growing worse, especially if all three have, it would be strange to call the result "development" even if per capita income doubled.

The characteristics of modern economic growth are ably summarized by Kuznets in his 1971 Nobel lecture.

First and most obvious are the high rates of growth of per capita product and of population in the developed countries – both large multiples of the previous rates observable in these countries and of those in the rest of the world, at least until the recent decade or two. Second, the rate of rise in productivity, i.e., of output per unit of all inputs, is high, even when we include among inputs other factors in addition to labour, the major productive factor – and here too the rate is a large multiple of the rate in the past. Third, the rate of structural transformation of the economy is high. Major aspects of structural change include the shift away from agriculture to nonagricultural pursuits and, recently, away from industry to services; a change in the scale of productive units, and a related shift from personal enterprise to impersonal organization of economic firms, with a corresponding change in the occupational status of labour. Shifts in several other aspects of economic structure could be added (in the structure of consumption, in the relative shares of domestic and foreign supplies, etc.). Fourth, the closely related and extremely important structures of society and its ideology have also changed rapidly. Urbanization and secularization come easily to mind as components of what sociologists term the process of modernization. Fifth, the economically developed countries, by means of the increased power of technology, particularly in transport and communication (both peaceful and warlike), have the propensity to reach out to the rest of the world – thus making for one world in the sense in which this was not true in any pre-modern epoch. Sixth, the spread of modern economic growth, despite its worldwide partial effects, is limited in that the economic performance in countries accounting for three-quarters of world population still falls far short of the minimum levels feasible with the potential of modern technology.[4]

It will be seen that Kuznets uses, in order of presentation, two aggregate economic variables, two structural transformation variables and two factors affecting the international spread of growth. Sustained growth in national output, an outcome of a long-term rise in capacity to provide a wide range of goods to its population, is the sign of economic maturity. Advancing technology is a precondition of continuous economic growth. Institutional, attitudinal and ideological adjustments are a must; without them technological innovations will be useless. Although the distributional spread of goods to the population is not clearly spelled out and Kuznets speaks only of structural adjustment not change, he does register a definite advance. In analysing the international spread of growth, he puts his finger on the main point.

It is against this background of the theory of economic development that we shall examine the major notes of dissent. But before doing so a brief reference to orthodox Marxist theory is necessary. The Marxist approach is also essentially evolutionist, and linear, involving a movement from primitive communism to the ultimate classless society. In this process capitalism is a necessary and even desirable stage, though the progress of humanity does not stop there. Relationships of production determine the nature of the social order and their inner contradictions force the movement of society to the next higher formation. Unable to resolve its inner contradictions the capitalist order will crack up to be replaced by the communist order which, being free from class contradictions, will be stable and permanent. Marx thus articulated a philosophy of history; he also provided an agenda for action and a prophecy for world's future. The idea of economic development was implicit in his view of social development. Though he also was Eurocentric in some ways, his formulation had a greater universal appeal. His latter day followers – the neo-Marxists – were to provide some excellent critiques of Western development theory.

Voices of Dissent

The developmentalists, representing the liberal Western stream of thought, are no longer heard with hushed and awed silence in the Third World. They are treated as false prophets whose faulty paradigms led to a massive misdirection of effort. The voices of dissent, that began as barely audible murmurs, have now acquired strength and assertiveness. The failure of the paradigm was, in the main, behind this multifarious dissent. Some who started as its enthusiastic supporters became disaffected and began to think about alternative strategies. Mao's thought, and especially the performance of the People's Republic of China, provided inspiration to many, including even some of those who had derided it earlier. There was also the belated rediscovery of Gandhi's economic philosophy in the context of the focus on poverty and generally in relation to the discussion on the crisis of industrial civilization. A third strand was introduced by independent-minded scholars of the Third World who, along with some like-minded Western colleagues, explored the inadequacies of the reigning paradigm, offered insightful critiques and developed alternative models.

The Pakistani economist Mahbub ul Haq, Cambridge and Yale educated and a World Bank official, represents the first strand. Of course, there are many others like him. Haq's admirable *The Poverty Curtain* (1976) is as important for its intellectual biographical vignettes as it is for its analyses (which present an excellent case study).[5] In the former aspect it presents an excellent case study. We hear him first (pp. 3–5) arguing the case for the Western model, gradually learning from experience, and as an ultimate *volte face* suggesting (pp. 27–8) that

1. Growth in GNP often does not filter down: what is needed is a direct attack on mass poverty.

2. The market mechanism is often distorted by the existing distribution of income and wealth: it is generally an unreliable guide to setting national objectives.

3. Institutional reforms are generally more decisive than appropriate price signals for fashioning relevant development strategies.

4. New development strategies must be based on the satisfaction of basic human needs rather than on market demand.

5. Development styles should be such as to build development around people rather than people around development.

6. Distribution and employment policies must be an integral part of any production plan: it is generally impossible to produce first and distribute later.

7. A vital element in distribution policies is to increase the productivity of the poor by a radical change in the direction of investment toward the poorest sections of society.

8. A drastic restructuring of political and economic power relationships is often required if development is to spread to the vast majority of the population.

Evidently others like Mahbub ul Haq have been tormented by the ferment within. They have chosen not to be as explicit about it.

The Mahatma (Gandhi) and Mao make strange company: one was a votary of non-violence, the other believed that power lay in the barrel of the gun; one was a believer, the other an atheist; one supported austerity as a way of life, the other chose it as a temporary expedient. But they had many similarities also. Both shared a concern for the common man, both believed in the dignity of labour, both advocated a philosophy of self-reliance and both opted for a self-limiting society. And both were great mass mobilizers for their cause.

Gandhian ideas rediscovered after years of neglect are relevant in the context of the debate on development for a variety of reasons. Gandhi had the vision to foresee the coming crisis of industrial civilization; his focus was on the poor and the deprived; he had definite ideas on technological choices and scale of production; he was an ardent advocate of self-reliance; his reflections on the nature of the community were important; he relied on mass mobilization as the principal instrument of social action; and finally, he gave primacy to a moral order – nationally and internationally. We do not have to read Schumacher, Illich, et al., to gauge his impact on alternative ways of thinking.

Mao, on the other hand, is distinguished for making an alternative style of development possible. Outside China his strategy was sneered at and ridiculed; it was contrary to all fashionable and accepted development thinking. None the less he made the impossible possible. To quote Mahbub ul Haq again,

> Within a period of less than two decades, China has eradicated the worst forms of poverty; it has full employment, universal literacy and adequate health facilities; it suffers from no obvious malnutrition or squalor. What's more, it was my impression that China has achieved this at fairly modest rates of growth, by paying more attention to the content and distribution of GNP. In fact, China has proved that it is a fallacy that poverty can be removed and full employment achieved only at high rates of growth and only over a period of many decades.
>
> How has it accomplished this? Of course, its political system, its isolation, its great size, its ideological mobilization, all of these have contributed to the evolution of its pattern of development. But are there any lessons to learn, even if we do not subscribe to its political system? Is there not a practical

illustration here of a selective attack on the problems of poverty, pursuit of a threshold income and minimum consumption standards, merger of production and distribution policies and achievement of full employment with a meager supply of capital? It is no use insisting that these results must have been achieved at tremendous social and political costs; people in the developing countries are often undergoing these costs without any visible economic results so that they look at the experience of China with great envy and praise. It is time, especially as China's isolation ends, that there be an objective and detailed study of its experience in place of the usual rhetoric to which we have been subjected so far.[6]

Now the four modernizations have taken over. They are perhaps an evolutionary necessity. It should be remembered, however, that foundations for them were laid by Mao. Gandhi's precepts and Mao's praxis both require serious analytical study.

Third World endeavours toward development have undergone at least three phases – imitative, reactive, and experimental. Currently, they are passing through the fourth, that of search. There was considerable overlap among the earlier phases and they do not necessarily represent linear progression. In the first phase Western ideas and models were uncritically adopted; some adaptations were made and a few elements were borrowed from the Soviet model. (The socialist countries, of course, were an exception.) In the reactive phase new ideologies were projected – African socialism, basic democracy, the Indian path of development and so forth. These had more rhetoric than substance; all that they did was to add a few diacritical marks to the existing paradigm of development. This phase was followed by experiments with different strategies – control, decontrol, import substitution, export promotion, industrialization, population control, community development and intensive agricultural development, poverty eradication, employment generation, and so forth. Currently the search is for a more viable, organically linked and comprehensive strategy of development.

The major issues in development theory from 1950 onwards have been ably and succinctly discussed by Björn Hettne in his small but perceptive *Current Issues in Development Theory* (1978) and some subsequent writings.[7] They have also emerged in clear relief in much of the recent debate on the subject; they do not require repetition here, where we will merely highlight some significant features of dissenting arguments. These are partly reactive, partly born out of new understanding of the empirical reality and partly a product of endogenous creativity and reflection.

A profile of what has come to be known as the international structuralist model can now be drawn.

1. Underdevelopment is a created condition, not the original state in the evolutionary process. The point is well argued by T. Dos Santos (1969).[8]

> Underdevelopment, far from constituting a state of backwardness prior to capitalism, is rather a consequence and particular form of capitalist development known as dependent capitalism . . . dependence is a *conditioning*

situation in which the economies of one group of countries are conditioned by the development and expansion of others. A relationship of interdependence between two or more economies or between such economies and the world trading system becomes a dependent relationship when some countries can expand through self-impulsion while others, being in a dependent position, can only expand as a reflection of the expansion of the dominant countries, which may have positive or negative effects on their immediate development. In either case, the basic situation of dependence causes these countries to be both backward and exploited. Dominant countries are endowed with technological, commercial, capital and socio-political predominance over dependent countries – the form of this predominance varying according to the particular historical moment – and can therefore exploit them, and extract part of the locally produced surplus. Dependence, then, is based upon an international division of labour which allows industrial development to take place in some countries while restricting it in others, whose growth is conditioned by and subjected to the power centres of the world.

2. Development does not necessarily travel from the centre to the periphery. On the contrary, as Paul Baran (1962) suggests, underdevelopment of the periphery is the result of the development of the centre.[9] The expansion of industrialized and capitalist nations creates and perpetuates underdevelopment. Thus, development and underdevelopment are two sides of the same coin. Andre Gunder Frank (1971) goes a step further to explain the development of underdevelopment and predicts that under the capitalist order underdevelopment is likely to be a permanent feature.[10]

3. Capitalist development creates a dualism both at the international and national levels. Superior and inferior relations are chronic; the distance between them actually goes on increasing. Interplay of a number of factors perpetuates this dependency relationship. The superior manipulate, to their advantage, world resource and commodity markets; have privileged access to scarce raw materials; and have the capacity to subvert the political structure and economic plans of the less developed countries. They are connected and have mutually reinforcing relations with the privileged élites of the Third World.

4. Intranational dualism within the Third World itself creates small centres of wealth and power while the periphery remains impoverished. The vast majority are only nominally benefited by development. The gap between the top 20% and the bottom 40% widens; the rich get richer; the pace of marginalization of the poor increases. The feudal structures change only minimally. The parasitic bourgeoisie does not, in this case, play its historical role of liberating the forces of production. Meaningful structural change is made difficult by the concentration of power in the hands of the thin "upper crust" and their alliance with powerful external patrons.

5. International aid is eye-wash. It feeds the Third World with false paradigms which are not intended to and cannot raise up the less developed – at any rate their masses – from backwardness. The exploitative policies of the developed countries – inappropriate transfers of technology, unequal

terms of trade and misdirected assistance – lead to the continued existence of underdevelopment. In the final analysis, so-called aid only strengthens dependency relationships.

6. Dependency has other harmful side effects. It leads to intellectual colonialism, irrelevant educational systems, and that of luring talented personnel, through attractive financial rewards, away from the less developed countries. The demonstration effect of high living in rich countries leads to misdirection of modernization in the Third World.

To sum up, the dependency syndrome ties the less developed countries into the domestic and international policies of the rich and powerful countries and subverts the possibility of their autonomous and endogenous development.

Such a brief presentation naturally cannot take account of all the major currents either in the *dependencia* school of thought or in the neo-Marxist critiques of development. It does not take adequate account either of the criticisms emerging in the West. They pose a challenge to the ruling developmental paradigm and represent an effort at indigenization of development thinking. The notions of *dependencia* (dependency), *indigenismo* (indigenization), *desarrollo hacia adentro* (inward looking development), and *marginalidad* (marginality) are important; but they do not add up to a universal theory of development or underdevelopment. Dependency explains a great deal but not all. All the ills of underdevelopment cannot be attributed to rich countries. In the first place, why did what is now the Third World lose out to expanding imperialism? Dependency theory can be an alibi for inaction. Is self-criticism not necessary? What correctives has the Third World devised in the last three decades? It should perhaps give some recognition, though grudging, to the small benefits that have accrued to it from Western domination in the form of infrastructure, organization and ideals. The continued economic growth in rich countries has enabled growth rates of output, in some less developed countries, which are much higher than in the past. This, as Singer (1970) argues, has a snag.

> The very forces which are set in motion by the rapid growth of the richer countries – specifically the development of even more sophisticated, costly and capital-intensive technologies, and of mortality-reducing health improvements and disease controls – are such as to create forces within the poorer countries – specifically a population explosion, rising unemployment and inability to develop their own technological capacities, which may in fact assure that they will *not* have the time needed for the continued maintenance of current growth rates, let alone their acceleration, so as to result in acceptable levels of development.[11]

The main questions that remain unanswered are, how to liberate the economy from dependency? And how to delink the centre from the periphery to bring about a more equal distribution of income?

Utopias for the Future: NIEO and Another Development

The future is a major concern of humankind. There is a global search for alternatives; building world models has become a minor scholarly industry. International fora, at different levels, are used to ventilate grievances, to strike bargains, and to argue and agitate for reordering the world economy in accordance with more just and equitable principles. The UN, through two significant resolutions, has articulated the need and sketched the guidelines for a New International Economic Order (NIEO). Among the most important contributions made by independent but like-minded experts are the "Cocoyoc Declaration" of 1974, the document produced by the *Third World Forum* of 1975, and the *North-South* report (1980) of the Brandt Commission. *What Now: Another Development* (1975), a report of Dag Hammarskjöld Foundation published to synchronize with the Seventh Special Session of the UN General Assembly, stands in a class by itself.[12] The comments that follow will be restricted to UN-supported NIEO and *What Now* – two outstanding examples; one official, the other unofficial.

UN documents are not expected to propound systematic theories; they can at best articulate an action-oriented consensus. Any consensus, especially one at the UN level, reflects pragmatic adjustments and compromises. Despite this limitation the two UN documents on the NIEO – 3201 (S-VI) and 3202 (S-VI) – have attracted wide attention and aroused some hope. In the barest outline the proposals are:

1. The less developed countries should concentrate on (and should be helped) increasing their production. This objective could be achieved by reorganizing the global system in such a way that all constituents stand to gain in the process. To this end they have to be integrated into the international market: industrialized countries have to reduce import tariffs, encourage the utilization of natural resources in developing countries by not using synthetics, and increase the quantum of development aid. The industrialization of the less developed countries has also to be supported by technology transfer and encouragement to export promotion.

2. Unequal distribution of wealth has to be attended to with a view to ensuring a rational, just and equitable order. The measures indicated are: fuller participation of the less developed countries in global economic decision making, better terms of trade, special agreements on raw materials, and a measure of control over multinational corporations.

3. Efforts should be made to promote collective self-reliance by encouraging the formation of regional markets within the Third World.

4. Producers' associations should be formed to manage the exploitation of natural resources and the redistribution of the wealth created from it.

This normative framework is a declaration of pious intentions which, if accepted, would make things somewhat better but would not bring about any structural change. Of course, the UN works under certain constraints: it can persuade, even pressurize, but not enforce its decisions. It has to recognize the sovereign equality of the member states and does not, in the normal course, interfere in their internal affairs. The integration of Third World economies into the international market, contemplated under the NIEO, is a measure of doubtful utility.

Another Development is a blueprint for a preferred future. It suggests a course of development that is need-oriented, endogenous, self-reliant, ecologically sound and based on structural transformation. It is aimed at meeting human needs, endogenously defined and with primary focus on those who have been deprived and exploited. It recognizes the importance of equality, freedom of expression, conviviality and creativity. Each society is left free to operate according to its values and cultures and articulate its own vision of the future. No universal model is to be imposed; each society can build its own. For development a society has to rely essentially on its inherent strength, although collective self-reliance is not ruled out. Rational utilization of the biosphere is built into the model: outer limits have to be respected and local ecosystems handled sensitively. From the little community to the global human community structural transformations will be needed to evolve participative decision-making mechanisms. Capacity for self-governance will have to be strengthened.

How all this is to be achieved has not been spelled out, but the ideas embodied in the framework compel attention and respect. What is more powerful than ideas?

Notes

1. Rostow, Walt W., *Stages of Economic Growth*, Cambridge, Cambridge University Press, 1961.

2. Myrdal, Gunnar, *The Challenge of World Poverty*, New York, Pantheon, 1970.

3. Seers, Dudley, *The Meaning of Development*, New Delhi, Eleventh World Conference of the World Society for International Development, 1969.

4. Kuznets, Simon, "Modern Economic Growth: Findings and Reflection", in Cyril E. Black (ed.), *Comparative Modernization*, New York, The Free Press, 1976.

5. Haq, Mahbub ul, *The Poverty Curtain: Choices for the Third World*, New York, Columbia University Press, 1976.

6. Ibid., p. 37.

7. Hettne, Bjorn, *Current Issues in Development Theory*, Stockholm, Swedish Agency for Research Cooperation with Developing Countries, 1978.

8. Santos, T. Dos, "The Crisis of Development Theory and the Problem of Dependence in Latin America", *Siglo*, vol. 21, 1969.

9. Baran, Paul, *The Political Economy of Growth*, New York, Monthly Review Press, 1962.

10. Frank, Andre Gunder, *Sociology of Development and Underdevelopment of Sociology*, London, Pluto Press, 1971.

11. Singer, Hans W., "Dualism Re-visited: A New Approach to the Problems of the Dual Society in Developing Countries", *Journal of Development Studies*, vol. 7, no. 1, October 1970.

12. *What Now: Another Development*, The 1975 Dag Hammarskjöld report on development and international cooperation, Uppsala, 1975.

4 Social Development: Human Needs and Quality of Life

A by-product of the contemporary debate on modernization and development has been a mini-terminological revolution. The usage of some established terms has altered beyond recognition; new terms are coined sometimes for effect and sometimes to communicate subtle nuances of meaning. The progressive replacement of the more conventional "economic development" by "social development" and the linking of it to notions of "human needs" and "quality of life", however, is not indicative only of a change in fashion; it represents a paradigm shift.

In the conventional sense, in earlier social science literature, the term social development was used almost synonymously with social evolution. The major stages in the evolution of human society, identified in a macro-sociological perspective, presented a profile of social development. The significant landmarks in this evolutionary sequence – savagery, barbarism, and civilization, the last divided into pre-industrial and industrial phases – signified important shifts in societal attributes and the emergence of new social formations. Many evolutionists implied a near universality and inevitability in these evolutionary sequences; the attainment of each successive stage was believed to register progress. Entire humankind was seen as moving towards the goal of civilization and was expected sooner or later to achieve it.

In more recent discussions the notion of social development has been detached from the evolutionary hypothesis and has focused on the questions of the satisfaction of human needs and improvement in the quality of life. The concept of social development is more comprehensive than economic development; it subsumes the latter, but aims at the attainment of certain wider social objectives and ideals. Neither these objectives and ideals nor the concept of social development itself have been rigorously defined. The dimensions of the concept are the subject of debate and some tentative formulations of the indicators of social development, as well as of the quality of life, are beginning to emerge.

It has been observed, and amply documented, that economic development, while it is undeniably necessary, can lead to certain undesirable consequences. It has to be geared to specific social objectives. Growth rates, GNP and per capita income figures are often deceptive; their facade hides the ugly realities of the impoverishment and degradation of sizable groups. Thus, it is time that instead of GNP we start thinking in terms of GNW (Gross National Welfare) and social development.

The new objective calls for:

1. A shift in emphasis from the individual to larger collectivities, encompassing the poor majority;
2. the redefinition of social goals in terms of the satisfaction of human needs and improvements in the quality of life;
3. the modification in strategies of planning and implementation to take account of the interface between economic and cultural objectives;
4. the creation of a redistributional institutional structure for the attainment of the new social objectives, and evolving a broad strategy for organizational and value change to ensure speedy attainment of the redefined social goals;
5. the formulation of indicators to evaluate social progress and to assess emerging social trends;
6. the setting up of monitoring mechanisms to ensure that growth levels are sustainable and at no point exceed the outer limits;
7. the anticipation of growth-related and other problems and preparedness to handle them quickly and effectively; and
8. the creation of an ethos in which it is possible to question and rethink the appropriateness and adequacy of existing social formations and to work towards their restructuring.

There are three major aspects to the emerging concept: normative, evaluative and operative. While the three are necessarily interrelated, each has its own complexities. To flesh out the ideal of social development it is essential to attend to all of them simultaneously.

It has been stated earlier that economic growth alone is generally socially inadequate. This is obviously so, even in some of the world's affluent countries. Increased national wealth, while solving some problems, also generates a wide range of baffling new problems. A solution to the problem of inequality remains to be found. As long as economic and social inequality persists, and continues to grow, development cannot claim to have achieved one of its major objectives.

The spiralling per capita consumption of world resources by the highly developed societies will sooner or later encounter severe limitations. First, the developing countries will demand levels of comparable affluence and consumption. Second, a reduction in the high consumption of the limited natural resources will be necessary because of the growing recognition of the hazards of resource exhaustion. Third, the dangers of ecological imbalances and atmospheric pollution will necessitate both a reduction in the speed of development and an innovative scientific and technological response to the challenge. These and other related problems have already generated some serious criticism of industrial society.

The developing societies are still facing the spectre of poverty on a mass scale; only small sections of them have attained consumption levels comparable to those of the developed countries. And poverty is not one problem; it is a series of interrelated problems. In general, the developmental efforts of these societies notwithstanding, they find that the gap between the developed and the developing countries is widening and they are afraid that as years go by it is likely to widen still more. Their élite, who are the trend-setters and reference model for the lower strata of society, follow or, at least seek to emulate, international styles of high living. Thus, despite their poverty, these societies also latently cherish consumerism and promote it where they can. This distorted perspective leads to lopsided priorities in development planning. Individual consumption for the few often takes precedence over investment in social services for the many. Production of luxury or even utility cars, owned and operated individually, results in giving low priority to the production of buses for mass transit. Luxury housing begins to get priority over schemes of public housing. TV, even if it is introduced ostensibly for mass education, becomes a status symbol because of its high cost and begins to neglect its target audience. High prestige hospitals become the preserve of the rich and the influential. New ways are found to articulate status differences. An artificial world of conspicuous consumption prospers, dazzling the masses in the process. The Third World is chasing a mirage. Failures in development performance lead to frustration and anger; vendors of instant solutions and unfailing panaceas are temporarily hailed as prophets. But prosperity continues to be elusive; the crisis of distribution intensifies. A thoughtless imitation of the model of affluent societies leads to the perpetuation of social injustice. Despite the rhetoric of socialism, societies become more inegalitarian. Some countries, China and Cuba for example, have successfully resisted the temptation; a few others have tried and failed; many have done no more than express pious hopes.

An institutional revolution, involving a radical value change, is needed in both the affluent and the non-affluent societies. The dimensions of the problems facing the two types of societies are different and they will, as such, have to choose different paths for solving their respective problems. However, both will have to redefine their social objectives and will have to opt for some self-limiting choices according to the dictates of their environmental imperatives and cultural predispositions.

Experience of three decades of relatively unproductive development activity in the Third World necessitates serious rethinking regarding the social objectives of planning and the strategies of implementation. Some major shifts in approach are indicated. These are: 1) from self-oriented values to society-oriented values; 2) from present orientation to a present/ future orientation; 3) from high consumption to relative austerity; and 4) from goods to services.

The counter-productive and dysfunctional aspects of high consumption are all too evident. The mounting revulsion against an unjust system of distribution will compel a thorough-going modification of the system. The ideal, for the Third World at any rate, is relative austerity. If an ethos favouring it is created, the emphases will shift from goods to services, from personal consumption to collective welfare. Rather than concentrate excessively on self-needs, the individual will tend to merge them with the needs of the wider society. A reawakened social consciousness will lay stress on a common and ordered way of life characterized by justice, equality and fair play. Over-concentration on immediate goals can have lethal effects in the long run. Thus, it will be essential to relate time-bound programmes to the desired future. This will involve a consideration of what makes human communities viable; anticipation of future needs; and the setting up of conflict resolving, consensus building and problem solving mechanisms.

The necessary steps for evolving a proper normative structure for social development and for evaluating the trends of change appear to be: a balanced and reliable assessment of the contemporary social situation; an in-depth examination of key problem areas; and scientific forecasts of possible trends. This can be done by developing a series of social indicators. The quantitative measurement of developments in major policy areas – distribution and range of inequality (especially in respect of food and housing), education, public health, public order and deviance, population growth, and so forth – is relatively easy; but their qualitative dimensions are difficult to handle. How can the inputs and outputs be qualitatively assessed? What should the priorities and scales of inputs be? Does the eradication of poverty mean only increase in incomes? Or do we also have to ensure that increased incomes are utilized in a desirable way? Are higher literacy rates and a quantitative increase in the number of those receiving advanced education a sufficient indication of social development? Or do we have to examine the qualitative aspects of education? Such questions arise for each significant policy area. The attainment of the stipulated social objectives such as the ethos of austerity, social cohesiveness and integration, satisfaction through non-material or psychic rewards and urge for excellence will be still more difficult to measure. Simple quantitative indicators, are instruments of limited utility and validity. To enhance their predictive and prescriptive powers it is essential to evolve techniques that translate quality into quantity. And this cannot be done without certain significant value assumptions.

A meaningful programme of social development, thus, will require a series of reliable social indicators. They will be invaluable for an accurate reporting on the contemporary state of society, identifying trends of change, anticipating impending problems and crises and suggesting policy leads and strategy modifications.

What is expected, then, is a transformation in the cognitive, cathectic and evaluative orientations of society. In other words, modes of perceiving, of determining what is pleasurable and of judging what is right, need radical change. The desired cognitive framework is implicit in the foregoing discussion; cathectic and evaluative changes necessarily have to follow if alterations in the normative structure are to have any meaning. The essential factor is that in the new ethos there should be a sense of joy and fulfilment in doing things for society and contributing towards its enrichment, even if this involves withholding self-gratification. Success should be judged not by what individuals have been able to do for themselves and their families, but by what they have contributed to community and society through special skills and competence. The evaluative criteria will judge social action and individual performance in terms of their social relevance and contribution to the social good. Naturally, individual consumption bordering on indulgence will be looked down upon and recognition and social approval will greet behaviour that is good for the society at large.

It is bound to be difficult to operationalise transformations of such magnitude because the system, as it exists today, at any rate in large parts of the world, is tilted towards self-gratification and personal consumption; but it is not impossible. All the great religions of the world and the major philosophical systems have emphasized the balancing and harmonization of self-regarding and other-regarding impulses; most of them have shown a marked preference for the latter. The range of human historical experience is replete with examples of situations in which self-gratification has been sacrificed to make way for what was considered to be socially good. Such deeds and choices have enjoyed greater social commendation and esteem than selfish indulgence. Within our own lifetimes some societies have made bold and brave attempts at such transformations through conscientization, politicization and mobilization – not entirely without success. If the new social order is to be ushered in, the virtues of patience and persistence will have to be cultivated. A change of such importance cannot be brought about in a day or even in a decade; what is essential is to begin the journey.

Social development, according to J.F.X. Paiva (forthcoming)

> has two inter-related dimensions – the first is the development of the capacity of people to work continuously for their welfare and that of society's; the second is the alteration or development of a society's institutions so that human needs are met at all levels especially at the lowest level, through a process of improving the relationships between people and socio-economic institutions, recognizing that human and natural forces are constantly intervening between the expression of needs and the means to attain them.[1]

He adds,

> In this process a balance is sought between quantitative and qualitative meeting of needs through changes in societal institutions and in the use of available resources. An essential concern of social development is therefore with social justice and in the equitable distribution of the fruits of development.

The aim of social development is ultimately to achieve a more humanistic society with institutions and organizations that will respond more appropriately to human needs.

What needs emphasizing is that the society should have a developed and effectively functioning self-regulatory mechanism so that individual greed and selfishness are held in check, without in the process stifling incentives and motivations or promoting social parasitism. The concept of social development certainly does not imply the conversion of individuals into cheerless automatons and spiritless robots; they must enjoy the freedom to articulate their ideas and be a part of the decision-making processes in society. What is being emphasized is that individual fulfilment should be through societal channels and that social good should have primacy in an individual's thought processes and lifestyle.

Human Needs: A Value Perspective

In formulating a model of human needs we must keep in mind the special nature of the human animal. Humanity has evolved from lower forms of life. Contemporary human life has many carry overs from its evolutionary heritage. We have animal ends, but realize them through cultural means. Nutrition, sex and procreation, nurture and upbringing of progeny, shelter and other forms of physical protection, which are all basic needs, are all ends that we share with other animals.

But here the similarity ends. We eat cooked food and our preferences contribute to a million different culinary styles. What is acceptable food to one society may be unacceptable to another. Some religious groups reject pork, others may reject beef and still others may reject all animal flesh. Dogs are edible in some cultures, not so in many others. Some form of nutrition, however, is necessary and should be both adequate and balanced. The gratification of the sex urge is an animal end; but human-beings have incest taboos and evolve complicated rules of endogamy and exogamy defining those whom they can marry and those whom they cannot. Gestation among human-beings is long drawn out, and the human female is relatively vulnerable during this stage. This vulnerability factor has been further enhanced by our cultural growth. Procreation therefore makes certain demands on forms of human social organization, necessitating one form or another of relatively stable domestic group. The human infant is also vulnerable and dependent; maturation takes place over a long period. The need to provide physical and social sustenance during this period also has important bearings on forms of human obligations and organization. Provision has to be made not only for physical survival but also for psychological and social support. Being born human is not a sufficient condition for becoming human; the latter requires a long process of socialization and education.

In dealing with human-beings, however, we must not confine ourselves only to a consideration of basic survival needs. The aesthetic component of human life is important. Even prehistoric people found fulfilment in songs and dances; they have left behind some remarkable cave paintings, several of which transcend the depiction of the immediate environment and demonstrate a free play of imagination and creativity. Early artefacts of everyday use had aesthetic as well as functional elements. Early craftworkers showed a sensitivity to form, pattern and colour. Figurines and statues, again dating back to early times, offer further proof of the aesthetic and creative urge. This dimension has to be kept in mind when conceptualizing human needs. Of all animals, people alone pray. This too adds a special dimension to life, making some form of spirituality essential. In sum, we have to take account of a bewildering variety of components that go into the shaping of the life of *homo sapiens*.

We must keep an additional factor in view. We think, we can create and innovate, we transmit our innovation and creation and others absorb and learn from it. We are the most educable of all animals. Both creativity and learning are supported by other components built into our bio-psychological make-up – the craving for positive response. We need acceptance, affection and recognition. Creativity and quick and efficient learning earn these in ample measure. While recognizing tradition as an important element of human life we should not ignore the prize attached to creativity and innovation (although these under certain situations involve severe penalties also).

We are a culture building animal. Culture is an adaptative and problem solving instrument *par excellence*, but while solving one set of problems it produces another. It has made life at once easier and more complicated. Human wants are graded hierarchically and modes of satisfaction also form part of a similar hierarchy. We cannot therefore stop at thinking in terms of human needs as simply the satisfaction of basic animal ends; gratification at other levels and in other forms is equally necessary. Human needs cannot be rigidly defined. They necessarily undergo changes and in a matter of two or three generations human perceptions as to what needs are basic can undergo a thorough transformation.

It is a paradox that two-thirds of humanity has still to struggle for the satisfaction of the most elementary of its basic needs. Thus, high priority has to be accorded to the satisfaction of minimum needs. From there, societies must move towards the satisfaction of other forms and levels of needs. These needs are culturally derived and defined; as such they are not unchangeable. They can be consciously changed to impart to them a social orientation and the quality of sustainability.

Quality of life would depend on conceptualizing the human need-structure in a new perspective and on making adequate provision for it. It is difficult to offer an inventory of needs that would respond adequately to diverse cultural demands and aspiration levels. In recent years several formulations of human needs, basic needs, minimum needs, and so forth, have been attempted; they converge considerably, although they vary in respect of their elegance and sophistication. One feature that is common to all these models is that they are intellectuals' conceptualization of the human need structure; they are not culture specific and do not reflect the needs articulated by particular societies or communities. A model, of course, is a heuristic device and does not have to approximate to empirical reality. For the present it is sufficient to achieve a measure of consensus with regard to human needs at this abstract level.

In any event, the need structure will include:

1. Survival needs, with provision for nutrition, shelter, clothing, gainful employment, preventive and curative medicine and protection of life and property.

2. Societal needs, involving creation of viable communities, promotion of community spirit and social cohesion, developing effective conflict resolving and consensus building mechanisms, and evolving and enforcing norms of social discipline.

3. Cultural and psychic needs, including provision for personal freedom and privacy, leisure and its creative utilization, and equal opportunity for advancement and overall development.

4. Welfare needs, including measures offering a fair deal to the weak, the disabled, the handicapped and the vulnerable.

5. Adaptive needs requiring mechanisms for scanning the social, cultural, psychological and physical environments as well as for identifying and affecting modifications necessitated by changes in them.

6. Progress needs involving sharpening of problem anticipating and problem solving capabilities, growth of scientific and technological research, and development of human engineering skills.

The survival needs will require a basic alteration in extant distributive values and the prevailing reward system. They will also require a curb on individual consumption and extension and enrichment of social services. The societal needs assume the growth of social consciousness, restructuring of statuses and roles, and an imaginative and determined human engineering effort with the accent on cooperation, consensus and discipline. The welfare needs seek to offer protection to the weak and the vulnerable. In operationalizing them care will have to be taken to ensure that they do not indirectly contribute to the growth of a parasitical section in the society.

The cultural and psychic needs cover difficult and slippery terrain. The effectiveness of programmes geared to them will be judged by their success in finding an alternative reward structure that de-emphasizes material gains. Even in a predominantly society-oriented value system it would be essential to ensure a high measure of autonomy for the individual, who must have a sense of personal worth and freedom to articulate and find fulfilment. Leisure is a necessity, but it can be used towards non- and anti-social ends. Promotion of channels for its creative and productive utilization is essential. These channels should provide for a diversity and wide range of interests. Adaptive and progress needs make three kinds of demands: skills in environmental surveillance, foresight regarding problems that are likely to emerge and the innovative capability to find solutions to them through scientific, technological and behavioural research. They require careful attention in order to provide a relatively problem free social order.

The new design for living, aimed at ensuring social development, is likely to encounter several difficulties. First, entrenched vested interests are likely to oppose the emergence of a new redistributive institutional structure that is the prerequisite to the implementation of the projected design for living. Second, value abandonment, value acquisition, value retargeting and the value implementation implicit in the scheme will not be easy: established value patterns are likely to assert and reassert themselves, sometimes at unexpected turns. In societies with ancient traditions and a long record of continuity, every misapplication of science and technology and each failure in management of social change is likely to generate atavistic tendencies. Prejudices developed over generations, are likely to find new rationalizations and enthusiastic promoters. Third, the absence of international consensus of human goals and mechanisms to defuse explosive tensions will pose serious threats to a smooth transition from the prevailing chaos to the happy equilibrium implicit in the desired new design for living.

Formidable as the difficulties are, they are not insurmountable. All human societies, to a lesser or greater degree, tend to adjust to reality. The inevitable has to be accepted: essential adaptations are made. But in an era bristling with contradictions and paradoxes – one in which the gap between aspiration and achievement is widening, where there is growing disenchantment with the established order which is showing every sign of cracking up, and when a point has been reached where large sections of the population have become ungovernable – reality adjustment in the normal course is no longer feasible. To avert the impending peril innovative processes addressing themselves to the crises of our time must be set in motion. Humanity has done so, on a smaller scale, several times in the past.

Contemporary problems are infinitely larger and more complex; they are beyond palliatives. Far reaching institutional and value changes are indicated. Purposive thinking and resolute social action alone can save the situation. Society's response will be positive if the manifest and latent dimensions of the contemporary crisis can be explained and a viable and convincing alternative is put before it. Our efforts in this direction must be a creative response to the challenges of the contemporary social reality. Egalitarianism and social justice are not impossible ideals; redesigning our future through institutional revolution and value transformation is well within the realm of possibility.

Quality of Life

Conceptual models of "quality of life" are a relatively recent phenomenon mostly associated with new thinking about the goals of development; but what constitutes a good or satisfying life has been the subject of thought ever since humanity developed cultures, and, within their framework, began functioning according to a scale of values. Anthropological studies of small-scale and relatively undifferentiated communities – commonly known as primitive tribes – present a wide diversity of ways in which human groups learn to relate to nature, society and the supernatural. They seek to understand and explain the reality surrounding them, even though a part of their understanding may be based on myth and legend, magic and supernaturalism. Despite the inadequacy of knowledge and the non-scientific character of their understanding of the physical, social, and cultural environment, these cultures have proved durable. Mighty civilizations have flowered and perished; but tribal cultures have endured. The notions of good, satisfying, and desirable lifestyles are implicit in their normative structures, schema of values and cultural emphases. Societies of larger scale and civilizations – small and large – have been more explicit in this regard. Their normative structure defines more clearly what is desirable and good, although each one of them has set tolerance limits and permits variations in goal definition and goal attainment. Many civilizations have succeeded in establishing a balance and harmony between people, nature, and society; some in their pursuit of a high quality of life have created conditions that ultimately led to their decay and disintegration. There has always been a certain gap between the desired and the desirable and it has been the endeavour of all social systems to bridge it; some have succeeded, other have failed.

The diffusion of Western ideas and ideals has over-emphasized materialism. This statement does not imply endorsement of the materialistic West, spiritual East stereotype; the spiritual dimension of Western civilization has to be recognized. So long as materialism is kept within bounds it is natural and even necessary. In fact, no great religion, philosophical system or civilization has neglected the material dimension of life. Difficulties arise when wealth is equated with happiness and consumption is regarded as the main indicator of satisfaction, and when even academic discussions begin to rationalize these notions. It is true that in formal articulation of values self-denial, renunciation and other-regarding impulses find prominent mention and in times of deep crisis societies act according to these normally neglected values and cheerfully undergo considerable hardships and sufferings. However, the reigning philosophy of consumerism has emphasized the importance of self-gratification and has in the process eroded consideration of the individual's responsibilities to the larger society. Any consideration of the quality of life, in order to be meaningful, has to take into account simultaneously the question of individual gratification as well as social needs. Over-emphasis on personal satisfaction will make the social order untenable and will create a disequilibrium in society which may be difficult to manage.

It is difficult to project a universally acceptable definition of quality of life or to formulate indicators to measure or evaluate it, for besides representing objective conditions it also implies subjective feelings. Both are historically determined and their cultural contexts are important. As a starting point the operational definition used in the UNESCO Report (1977) appears satisfactory.[2] It says:

QOL is an inclusive concept which covers all aspects of living including material satisfaction of vital needs as well as more transcendental aspects of life such as personal development, self-realization and a healthy eco-system.

Mallmann (1977) refines the concept further and offers a more sophisticated definition:[3]

> It is a concept which refers to individuals, but determined, like aspirations, by the dynamic interaction between a given individual, his society and his habitat. Since it is determined by the satisfaction of aspiration, it ought to be analysed by at least the same number of dimensions as those which make up the human space ... The number of dimensions of human space is determined by the minimum number of independent needs with which the particular set of aspirations of any individual may be explained.

Evidently, individuals cannot be ignored in any consideration of the question of quality of life; their needs and their satisfactions are important. But it is necessary to remember that human individuals are very much creatures of their culture and their satisfaction and fulfilment can never be detached from the goals and instrumentalities of the social order which make them possible. The overall consideration of the quality of physical environment is also equally important as it is a determinant, to a significant degree, both of the objective conditions and subjective satisfactions of the individual. Thus, any satisfactory definition of the quality of life must include three diverse sets of criteria in their dynamic interaction: culturally-determined particularistic criteria, scientifically-determined universalistic criteria and criteria considering both environmental over-exploitation and degradation on the one hand and improvement on the other.

As new bridges of understanding are built societies and cultures will inevitably come closer and the base of interaction among them is enlarged. But culture diversity will persist as the homogenization of all societies and all cultures is neither desirable nor possible. Thus, cultural definition and evaluation of components of the quality of life, will never cease to be significant. At the same time, it should be emphasized that what is culturally right may not always be scientifically right and what is recommended by science may be culturally unacceptable. Modern science and technology cause modifications in historically and culturally derived notions and practices, but this process of adaptation is not always easy. For example, science can lay down the norms regarding the essential ingredients and quantity of nutrition; but in what form it is to be taken can best be left to individual cultures. This applies to most other areas of life.

In the final analysis quality of life is defined as a balance of satisfaction of the biological, derived and integrative needs of people in their social settings. The table that follows presents some of the more important requirements of a preferred quality of life on the individual and societal levels.

Table 4.1
Human needs and quality of life requirements

Needs/Requirements

Survival:
At individual level:
Adequate nutrition, including ready access to uncontaminated water supply.
Adequate housing.
Adequate clothing.
Access to preventive and curative medicine.
Security of life and property.
Gainful employment.

At societal level:
Organization of food security/production and distribution systems; supply of clean water.
Housing schemes for low income groups.
Organization of production/distribution systems for clothing.
Organization of network of medical facilities.
Security and police.
Employment schemes.
Mass education; covering areas of nutrition, water use, child care and health care.
Management of the environment.

Societal:
At individual level:
Sustenance from infancy to adolescence.
Socialization mechanisms.
Control mechanisms.
Sense of participation.
Opportunities for receiving positive response—reward and recognition.
Harmonizing individual and social needs.

At societal level:
Access by all to at least minimum sustenance needs.
Adequacy and consistency of socialization processes.
Unambivalent norms and their universalistic enforcement.
Growth of participative institutional structure.
Multilevel reward/recognition system for individual achievement and contribution to society.
Promotion of egalitarian ethos and recognition of primacy of social needs.

Cultural and Psychic:
At individual level:
Personal freedom, consistent with social needs.
Leisure and opportunities to use it productively.
Access to enjoyment of the products/achievement of culture.
Opportunities to make an individual contribution to above point.
Sense of personal worth.
Opportunities for personal advancement.

At societal level:
Promotion of an ethos of tolerance of cultural and religious differences, and upholding of legitimate personal freedom.
Organization of useful leisure time activities.
A policy for the promotion and dissemination of culture and the arts.
Promotion/recognition of excellence.
Multilevel and multifaceted opportunities of lifelong education.

Welfare:
At individual level:
Being able to overcome man-made deprivations and discriminations.
Being able to lead useful life despite natural or accidental handicap.

At societal level:
Abolition of discriminatory practices based on gender, race, religion, with special attention to degraded and culturally deprived groups.
Special schemes for the mentally and physically handicapped.
Affirmative action for above two points.

Adaptive:
At individual level:
Sense of history.
Awareness of forces shaping the modern world.
Predisposition to adjust quickly and smoothly to changes in the physical and socio-cultural environment.
Constructive social criticism.

At societal level:
Education for raising consciousness.
Effective communication strategies for adaptive change.
Developing social indicators and conduct of regular social audit.
Advance warning systems regarding impending crises.
Continuous modification of institutional structures.

Progressive:
At individual level:
Urge to explore, arrive at new understanding, and disseminate the implications of this knowledge.

At societal level:
Exploration of new frontiers of knowledge in science and technology, humanities and social sciences, with accent on application of findings for progress.

It will be seen that the notion of quality of life has been related to a tentative formulation of human needs presented earlier. Such a formulation implies very substantial changes in the normative and evaluative orientations both at the level of the individual and at the societal/cultural level. It has been demonstrated that the survival imperative is capable of inducing considerable flexibility in the ideas and attitude of humankind. In conceptualizing quality of life for the world's poor generally, and for the majority in the Third World particularly, the basic question is one of survival. Humanness demands a little more than physical survival. That is why the formulation involves consideration of what we may call survival plus—a cultural minimum over and above the biological minimum to accommodate aspirations and fulfilments that mark humans out from other animals. The formulation is not over-optimistic. The faith implicit in it, again, rests on our educability and our capacity to adjust to reality.

Notes

1. Paiva, J.F.X., "The Dynamics of Social Development and Social Work", in Daniel S. Sanders, (ed.) *The Developmental Perspective in Social Work*, University of Hawaii Press, forthcoming.

2. UNESCO, *UNESCO'S Policy Relevant Quality of Life Research Programme*, Paris, Unesco, 1977.

3. Mallmann, C.A., *The Needs and Processes, Goals and Indicators*, Paper submitted for the GPID project of the United Nations University, 1977, mimeo.

5   Parameters of Policy

The reigning paradigms of modernization and development no longer inspire the confidence which they did three decades back. Critical assessment of results and fresh endogenous reflection, have led to serious doubts and questions, which in their turn have thrown up insights and have led towards the emergence of an alternative paradigm. The broad configuration of the desired model is clear, although there is no unanimity in respect of the means by which to achieve it.

The Alternative Paradigm

A consensus about the new paradigm appears to be emerging.

1. While economic growth is necessary, *per se* it does not constitute development. It has to be linked to a set of well defined human – social and cultural – objectives. Economic growth has to be understood as an instrument of human development. It should first be able to meet the basic needs of the people at large and then move on to improving and enriching their quality of life.

2. Economic growth can no longer be defined merely as raising the GNP and per capita income. Both are necessary, but without a purposive orientation they can defeat the objectives of development. A major share of the benefits of growth is invariably cornered by the thin upper crust of society, leaving the masses where they were or worse off. The development paths so far followed by most Third World countries have proved blind alleys. The focus has to be on people and society. It implies more equitable distribution of goods and services. Experience suggests that this would lead to the acceleration of growth. Basic investment in people coupled with distributive justice is thus necessary. This investment must not lead only to individual betterment, but to enlarging and sharpening society's capability to come to grips with its problems and find effective solutions.

3. To be able to achieve these objectives fundamental structural change

is necessary. This necessity has been emphasized and reiterated several times; but in most Third World countries the efforts at structural transformation have been feeble and fall far short of what the situation demands. The direction of change in the personality system, the value attitude system and the social system have been spelled out with a fair degree of precision, but how societies should go about achieving these changes is not as clear. Education, the mass media and urbanization help, but only so far. The structure of economic opportunity has to be opened up and imaginative efforts must be made to rectify injustices of the past. This cannot be done without major alteration in the relationships of production, a conscious policy of positive discrimination and conscientization of the masses.

4. The development endeavours of the last three decades have been largely emulative and, therefore, in many instances misdirected. Of course, there have been ritualistic concessions to history and tradition, but invariably endogenous creativity has been held in check. A small élite – often with a Western orientation – has taken major decisions in respect of the present and the future; the people themselves having little say in them. The institutional structure of society permits them limited freedom to shape their own destinies. Many Third World countries are under authoritarian and repressive regimes, some have only a facade of democracy; where democracy still survives in the political sense, the choice of the people is restricted to one or the other élite-led political party whose orientations differ only in minor detail. To ensure endogenous growth a new institutional framework, assigning more decisive roles to the people and their associations, is necessary.

5. Steps have to be contemplated to make the process of development genuinely participative. This can be achieved only when people have real, not notional, access to power and resources. A democracy merely characterized by periodic elections is not truly participant. The people's initiatives should not be thwarted and mass mobilization should not be conceived only in terms of mass compliance in respect of decisions taken at centres of power dominated by the élite. In other words, people must not only decide for themselves what concerns their present and future, they should have the upper hand in implementing the development programmes.

6. The development process, almost globally, has shown a lack of sensitivity to the environment. This has had lethal effects. History bears testimony to the fact that some civilizations have died because of their reckless exploitation of the environment. Belatedly the West has awakened to the need to handle it more sensitively. A mistaken notion prevails in most Third World countries that because of their low levels of industrialization they do not face any major environmental hazards. This is not true. Environmental consciousness has to be promoted in the developing societies also, so that they can take timely steps to conserve and improve their environment. The environmentalists' warnings can only with grave consequences be written off as a passing fad.

7. An important element that is missing from most planning and

development is sustainability. Most developing countries are consciously or unconsciously trying to copy the West without any awareness of their resources and limits. It is evident that even the affluent countries have reached a point where their development, in some ways at least, is unsustainable and is resulting in mounting crises. Recession, inflation, unemployment, environmental hazards and so on are evidence of this. Third World countries have consciously to make their development sustainable; their ambition should not be pitched too high. This does not mean, however, that they should accord low priority to science and technology. Scientific and technological progress can be major determinants of sustainable development.

8. Third World countries should endeavour to make their development as self-reliant as possible. The basic idea here is to cross the dependency barrier and break the patron–client relationship with the more developed countries. Self-reliance is, however, a relative concept. Resource constraints, demographic equations and stages of scientific/technological progress are important variables governing possible degrees of self-reliance. Large and populous countries like China and India can be more self-reliant than small landlocked or island countries. The emphasis, therefore, should be on *attainable* degrees of self-reliance.

9. While relative self-reliance is the ideal, global interdependence cannot be ignored. The developed countries have depended, and still depend, on the developing countries for many important resources that have made their development possible and contribute to its continuation. This interdependence is not restricted only to raw and semi-processed materials; the West has drawn heavily also on the brain power and trained competence of the Third World. What is disconcerting is that much of this interdependence operates on such unequal terms. This is what the demand for a New International Economic Order is about. While the nuances and subtleties of the contemplated NIEO will continue to be debated and consensus reached by steps and stages, Third World countries must begin thinking in terms of pooling their competence and resources to find answers to their own problems. This cooperation and interdependence can be envisioned at several levels, encompassing sub-regional and regional groupings as well as the entire Third World. These patterns will have to be consistent with national honour and dignity as well as needs and economic rationality. At the same time patterns of global cooperation and interdependence also will have to be worked out. Enlightened self-interest coupled with the imperatives of survival and progress will with luck lead to the emergence of equity.

10. Another feature of Third World planning and development is their excessive concern with the present and lack of planning for the future. It is true that the needs of the present are many and complex; but it is dangerous to neglect the future. We should not push into the background in the name of pragmatism issues and problems that may assume frightening proportions in the future. It is essential to build into the development process orientation towards the future.

Although the need for a new paradigm of development, incorporating most of the elements discussed above, is deeply felt and unambiguously articulated, development practice shows little impact of the new thinking. Planning continues to have an élite bias; a small section determines what is good for the society and in the process gives high priority to what is good for itself and its own class interests. Poverty is recognized as the major problem, but this recognition has become almost ritualistic. It is the current fashion to speak in the name of the common people; but what they really get are a few crumbs of development. There is a reluctance to carry out meaningful and far reaching structural reforms. Many of the so-called reforms are meaningless and the complexities and loopholes built into them are so many and so diverse that the majority can at best benefit from them only marginally. A substantial part of development activity, despite populist postures, continues to be weighted in favour of the small privileged minority which deftly manipulates the levers of powers. And, by and large, planning objectives and processes continue to be emulative and exogenous, and therefore, misdirected. They are non-participative, evince low sensitivity to the environment and are in most cases unsustainable. In the absence of the requisite political will, and because of the perverse international climate and pressures, the ideal of self-reliance remains confined to rhetoric; in actual practice, dependency patterns continue to prevail. There is a wide gulf between the new thinking and the on-going praxis.

Why is there this glaring contradiction between thought and action? Evidently the power of entrenched vested interests is a factor to contend with. At the same time mounting pressure from the people wins them a few concessions here and there, now and then. In consequence, the Third World generally has the paradox of an intellectual and emotional awareness of the problems of the majority, but a near total lack of sensitivity and resolute political will to do something about them. The politics of pragmatism turn into a series of fire-fighting operations. Application of soothing salve proves a temporary expedient and does not provide the cure to the deep-seated malady. The people at large continue to rely excessively on the government, whose performance capability is eroded with every passing decade. A point has been reached when there is a paralysis of government, where most governments are perplexed and helpless in the face of their inability to cope with problems of growing complexity and magnitude. This leads to the inevitable conclusion that to be operationalized the new paradigm requires a new domestic order as well as a new international order. Unless the prevailing pernicious connections between the two traditional orders is broken, no fundamental change is possible, yet nothing short of fundamental change can meet the compelling demands of the alternative model of development.

Key Issues in Development Policy

The new paradigm of development calls for an alternative policy framework. If the development performance of the Third World has been unimpressive, the failure should be attributed to the absence of fit between the emerging paradigm and the institutional structure determining policy and its implementation. The traditional approach to policy simply does not respond to the needs implicit in the projected alternative model.

Determination of Goals

Even a cursory examination of the development plans of Third World countries will bring home the realization that the emphasis in them continues to be on growth or raising GNP. Notions of social development and the objectives of eradicating poverty and improving the quality of life are also beginning to be incorporated into these documents; but they invariably take a low priority and are not organically linked to the growth objectives. Thus, while the output goals are articulated in precise terms, the expression of cultural goals remain fuzzy and amorphous. Order is a precondition of continuing growth, but the order goals are also rarely considered as an essential ingredient of planning endeavours. It is necessary that we take into account cultural and order goals and their organic linkages alongside output goals. The former will provide a social purpose for economic growth and the latter make for conditions propitious to it.

Another flaw in the determination of goals is the excessive concern displayed for problems of the present and the obfuscation of long-range objectives. The present is no doubt important, but inept handling of it, though offering temporary relief, may create complex problems for the future which can assume insoluble proportions if they are not anticipated. Long-term planning is being introduced into an increasing number of Third World countries, but it has a subservient role and rarely makes a positive impact on contemporary plans. It is good to see that long-range concerns enter into the planning of environment and resources, but the human and social dimension still does not enter into them enough. As a consequence we may have, sooner rather than later, human and social/cultural problems that defy technological and management capability to handle them effectively. The signs are there for anyone to see, but what can be seen today is only the tip of the iceberg. Alternatives are not only a theme to be contemplated; we should begin acting on them now.

It has been observed that in the articulation of development goals politicians often present utopias which are beyond realization. This is a myopic way of handling development. They may be over-optimistic or may have only short-term political gains in view. This creates rising expectations which, when not met even partially, leads to mounting frustrations. Development goals, therefore, need to be searchingly examined for their viability and sustainability. Non-viable plans constitute opportunities lost and resources wasted; unsustainable development is worse. Both result in frequent policy changes which are confusing and are non-productive.

The Question of Limits

The concept of outer limits is of relatively recent origin.

It was generally used in a global context to suggest the fragileness of major planetary life support systems and processes in much the same way that the concept of 'spaceship earth' suggested the finiteness ... of the planet on which man is totally dependent for his survival (Matthews, 1976).[1]

Further reflection on and deeper examination of the concept reveals its complexity; simplistic definitions do not help. To illustrate the point we have to return to the seminal essay by William H. Matthews quoted earlier. Its succinct conclusions merit reproduction in full.

There are two basic determinants of outer limits: (a) the quantity of existing resources and the laws of nature; and (b) the way man conducts his activities with respect to this natural situation. Both of these must be known before outer limits can be defined for most renewable resources and environmental systems. For non-renewable resources only the first determinant is operative. Even with complete scientific understanding of biophysical conditions, more information would be required about societal values, priorities and decision-making processes if most outer limits are to be defined.

The word 'outer' in the phrase 'outer limits' refers to the context or frame of reference within which the limits are considered; for example, 'global' outer limits, 'national' outer limits and 'regional' outer limits.

The choice of contexts for various outer limits has major implications with respect to the way they will be defined both scientifically and through societal and political processes.

The choice of contexts is an important factor when dealing with issues of independence, dependence and interdependence. The goal of meeting basic human needs without transgressing outer limits seems to imply a set of priority decisions that have probably not been made explicitly by many societies. There are so many societal decisions that influence the definition of outer limits that the objective of not transgressing outer limits can mean very different things even if the scientific content is the same.

The objective of not transgressing outer limits can be interpreted as attaching a condition of 'sustainability' on meeting needs but the definition for this is also subject to many societal decisions.

In reality the objective of not transgressing outer limits probably must be considered as one more (albeit a very important one) set of values to be considered in societal decision-making. This will require a careful development of criteria for considering resource and environmental issues. Integrating the concept of outer limits into societal decision-making will require careful examination of the nature and limitations of societal and political processes to utilize scientific information, to deal with cultural differences, to institutionalize needed procedures and to utilize relevant technologies.

The acquisition of existing scientific data and a survey of scientific opinion on various outer limits is a straightforward, though not necessarily easy, task. In many cases, however, this will not be sufficient for even preliminary estimates of outer limits both because of the paucity of data and because of the importance of non-scientific factors.

There are several major methodological problems which must be overcome before the primarily technical approaches can be fully developed. These include the determination of 'building blocks' of analysis, the regressive nature of the 'building blocks', the great variety of alternative strategies for meeting a particular need, the additive impacts and demands of all activities, and the development of adequate information bases and models for detailed analyses.

The question of outer limits relates mainly to population, food, energy and other essential resources. The doomsday prophesies of the Malthusians and the neo-Malthusians have already proved false; world food production has caught up with the rise in population and is marginally ahead of it. The margin is still narrow and the situation continues to be precarious; but it is not one without hope if human ingenuity can be galvanized towards solving the problems posed by population and food ratios. According to one estimate the land resources of the world can provide food to sustain a population of 36 billion. There is a snag, however; the projection presupposes development of the capability to desalinize sea water, pump it long distances and lift it to considerable heights at low cost for irrigation and power generation. Another projection, from the Linnemann group, suggests that 3.5 billion hectares are cultivable and can be made to yield an annual harvest of 50 billion tons of food, representing roughly forty times more production than today. Mineral resources supply can be increased, though at enhanced unit cost; pollution can be controlled and environmental quality improved, if 2% of the total world Gross National Product could be ploughed into these programmes. Science and technology are capable of finding functional analogues for rapidly depleting resources, if the requisite massive financial inputs are made and we allow for a gestation period. As new frontiers of science and technology open up, the prospects of deriving resources even from outside the earth become brighter. Our planet's resources may be finite; but human capability to augment them or find substitutes is infinite.

While the outer limits have to be kept in view, it is the inner limits that pose the most vexatious problems. The parameters of these limits are set by social and political factors as well as institutions and cultures. While we talk about the need for greater food production, we drag our feet when it comes to changing the structure of land ownership. Accelerated development is possible but it will need massive inputs. According to one estimate such inputs would be of the order of 35% of a country's GNP. The least developed and even the developing countries can hardly raise the resources to do so; belts cannot be tightened beyond a point. It would be futile to look for resources transfer of this magnitude from the developed world; they will not put aside even 1% of GNP. Their contribution has been slightly higher than 0.3%, but has never touched 0.4%. Science and technology make breathtaking advances, but their applications are expensive and it will be many decades before even a fraction of the new discoveries reach the countries which need them the most. In any case we have to recognize the time lag between the pressure of needs and the scientific and technological solutions to them. Glorious utopias can be projected for the year AD 2500; but it is difficult to motivate the present generation to toil and sacrifice for such a remote future when the present is so hard. And who knows about the future? Our folly may lead to an Armageddon which may annihilate our species.

The inner limits are also important because accelerated progress meets with unpredictable reactions. A telling case is that of Iran, where the deposed Shah Mohamed Reza Pahlavi started a programme as early as 1943 to ensure bread for everyone, housing for everyone, clothes for everyone, hygiene for everyone and education for everyone. He introduced agrarian reforms, expanded the educational base, set up a public health delivery system, sought to bring about the White Revolution, carried out administrative reforms and launched action to secure women's emancipation. These were worthy development objectives and met nearly all the criteria of modernization and economic rationality. The results were impressive. In a quarter of a century there was something of a miracle in terms of growth rates. According to organizations linked with the UN, the annual rate of economic development in Iran since the beginning of the White Revolution was 13%. The average wage registered an impressive upward rise from under $160 to $2,200 per capita by the beginning of 1978. According to Iranian figures it was higher still – $2,540 per capita. The then Shah even claimed that the growth rate in Iran was four times that of Japan in 1975. These claims may have been exaggerated but the interesting point is the dramatic collapse of the regime and its programme. The breakdown of modernization in this case can be attributed to the inner limits – constraints of social structure and cultural values and of course of outside pressures impinging on Iran's economy and polity. Thus, a consideration of the limits of economic rationality has to form part of the understanding of inner limits.

A policy framework for development must take into account a country's population and available resources. Our fears of a population explosion may prove to be false and in the long run population may prove to be an asset. Today, however, numbers still constitute a problem. Population growth rates have to be checked and by investment in man its quality has to be improved. Similarly, development policy has to consider efficient resources utilization as well as provide for their maintenance, enhancement, and substitution.

Preservation and improvement of environmental quality is yet another important factor. We owe it to our generation and to the succeeding generations that the environment is not so polluted and degraded that it becomes a survival hazard. Endogenous creativity can find ways for effective utilization of local resources and in selected areas can promote appropriate technology, ensuring against environmental losses and resource exhaustion. Dependency in the field of science and technology is perhaps worse than political and economic dependency. What the Third World needs is the right mix and balance of high intermediate and small-scale technology. Technology can be borrowed and adopted, it can be adapted, but its indigenous growth is essential. There is no short cut to meeting the challenge of outer limits. That still leaves us with the problem of inner limits which becomes increasingly complicated because of the pressure of conflicting interests from within and from without. Structural change within, at a sustainable pace and in an acceptable direction, is necessary. At the same time efforts must be made to establish a sane and rational international order.

Structural Change

What happens when an irresistible force meets an immovable mass? Philosophers have not been able to resolve the question; but in the context of development this question has acquired immediacy. If we are serious about development, especially eradication of poverty, improving the quality of life and reducing the income disparities, the need for structural change is irresistible, but the core of the structure, during the last three decades, has proved intractable and immovable. The result is an impasse, blocking both balanced development and just distribution of its products. The stalemate has caused much unnecessary travail. The series of avoidable traumatic shocks emanating from it may lead the world from disequilibrium to destruction. Hesitant action will only make the situation worse; any meaningful policy framework, therefore, has to provide for structural change, making it as smooth, painless, and free of injuries as possible.

To put it briefly, and somewhat bluntly, thorough-going changes in the relationships of production are indicated. This may sound like the repetition of a Marxist cliche, but non-Marxist options for realizing the envisioned objectives are open. South Korea's much lauded economic miracle can be attributed in fair measure to its land reforms and investments in human capital formation. Whatever the path of development a country adopts, people–land relationships have to change. To achieve this a bloody revolution is not necessary; resolute land reforms can attain the desired goal. The longer these are delayed, the more attractive the alternative of a revolution becomes. The prospects of redistribution of land are less alarming than some people make them out to be. Global experience suggests that smaller but viable holdings can contribute to raising agricultural productivity. Collectives and cooperatives have also achieved the same results, although setting them up and making them work has not always been easy. The gains are not to be measured only in economic terms of increased productivity; the psychological dimension, contributing to an enhanced sense of human worth, is also important. Unutilized or under-utilized land can gradually be worked to full capacity and, in the process, a more equitable distribution of income can be ensured.

Similarly, the patterns of industrial management have to be made more participative. Here also several viable options are open and several advantages can be foreseen. First, participation will lead to greater industrial peace and discipline by ensuring rational collective bargaining. Participation will also lead to added productivity. Participation plus equitable wages would have some other advantages, such as contributions by the labour force towards evolving cost-efficient techniques. Measures of structural change should attempt to narrow the gap between income disparities and through participation raise productivity in a relatively cordial atmosphere. The much talked about work ethic cannot be brought about unless structural transformations are introduced. The major policy issue in this area is to adopt, or better still evolve, the right model and make it work.

Making structural changes work involves also the question of strategy and tactics. From Scandinavia to Vietnam there are several models of egalitarian societies. The Scandinivian countries adopted an evolutionary path, the USSR and China attained their objectives through revolutions. In some societies communism has a more human face than in others. A great deal can be done through the democratic process by purposive and resolute legislation, supported by efficient implementation as well as effective communication. Revolutions cannot be ruled out, at least as a court of last resort. Repressive regimes and myopic and effete democracies often pave the way for them. The notion of revolution, however, has to be demystified. Revolution is a long and painful process, it is not magic. Romantic adventurism does not lead to successful revolutions. Conditions have to be right and a determined leadership and dedicated cadres have to be there to implement plans in a manner that brings visible results within a decade. Evolutionary or revolutionary, both paths imply certain human costs. Obstinate entrenched interests can create conditions of anarchy and confusion by being insensitive and unresponsive to popular urges. Mindless revolutionary zeal and premature action produce similar results. Both result in the erosion of cherished values and may lead to the emergence of authoritarian and dictatorial regimes. Recent history bears ample testimony to this.

The general direction of structural change has been indicated above. Fixation of proximate goals and determination of the pace for their attainment, however, will have to be done through appropriate and cautious tactics that work; pragmatism cannot be ruled out in this context. This applies equally both to evolutionary and revolutionary alternatives. Beliefs and special cultural sensitivities have to be respected and institutions of society cannot be bulldozed and rebuilt in a decade. Social change takes three generations or more to stabilize and an unseemly haste is likely to prove counter-productive and self-defeating. Iran's quick march from the oil age to the atomic age and its ultimate collapse are a telling case in point. People cannot be driven, they have to be taken along; better still they should themselves determine where they are going and at what pace they would like to move. The view that tradition is a barrier to modernization and development is no longer accepted. It has enough reserves of vitality to adapt itself to the changing milieu and set new directions for the attainment of progress. Pragmatism should not be permitted, however, to dilute ultimate objectives, although a few strategic retreats may be found inevitable and even justifiable. Flexibility and perseverance have to be built into the policy processes.

No simplistic solutions to the question of structural change are possible. This is a problem area which taxes the ingenuity of the policy planner to the utmost. Implementation of even the most well intentioned policies meet with stiff resistance from entrenched interests. The recent history of the Third World is replete with examples of how these interests have sabotaged land reforms and subverted other measures aimed at structural transformation. This has been the experience of India, Pakistan and Bangladesh. Nor do power interests from outside hesitate to add fuel to the flames. In the cynical and amoral order that prevails today everything is possible. Those who speak in the name of human rights and profess democratic ideals have not hesitated to subvert democracy in some Third World countries and form curious but convenient alliances with dictatorial regimes that have no regard for human rights or democracy. The calculus of power prevails over considerations of ideological compatibility or human compassion. These obstacles notwithstanding, structural change still remains an imperative prerequisite for successful development.

Population–Food–Energy Nexus

In the recent dialogues on development, population as a variable in the development process has been somewhat underplayed. It is true that many pessimistic prophesies such as "if the population continues to explode, many people will starve", "all of the major environment problems can be traced to too many people", and "without drastic intervention to check the geometric growth of population there will soon be standing room only" have not stood the test of time. There have been some serious errors in demographic forecasts and projections of future population growth. Malthus, writing in 1798, was wrong in his theory that population would outstrip food supply. His error was that he saw eighteenth-century technology as a constant and could not imagine the major breakthroughs that would come about by continuous application of science and technology to agriculture. In the late 1960s the neo-Malthusians went wrong in forecasting a global famine because their projections were based on early 1960s technology. A strong current of thought now holds that mankind can control its destiny – the technological constraint is likely to result in lowering of population growth and modern science and technology will register unprecedented advances to meet the challenge of world hunger. In the long term this optimism may be justified; but the contemporary context still raises some doubts and fears. According to the UN Fund for Population Activities the best demographic estimates of world population at the turn of the century, in 1976, was set at nearly 7 billion. The *Global 2000 Report to the President* estimate is close to it; from 4 billion in 1975 world population is likely to rise to 6.35 billion in 2000. This would represent an increase of more than 50%. The picture, therefore, does not appear to be very rosy. If 75 billion people were added to world population in 1975, nearly 100 million would be added each year in 2000. What is significant and ominous in this context is that nearly 90% of this growth will take in the poorest countries. Table 5.1 spells this out.

Table 5.1
Population projections for world, major regions and selected countries (millions)

	1975	2000	Per cent increase by year 2000	Average annual per cent increase	Per cent of world population in year 2000
World:	4,090	6,351	55	1.8	100
More developed regions	1,131	1,323	17	0.6	21
Less developed regions	2,959	5,028	70	2.1	79
Major regions:					
Africa	399	814	104	2.9	13
Asia and Oceania	2,274	3,630	60	1.9	57
Latin America	325	637	96	2.7	10
USSR and Eastern Europe	384	460	20	0.7	7
North America, Western Europe, Japan, Australia and New Zealand	708	809	14	0.5	13
Selected countries and regions:					
People's Republic of China	935	1,329	42	1.4	21
India	618	1,021	65	2.0	16
Indonesia	135	226	68	2.1	4
Bangladesh	79	159	100	2.8	2
Pakistan	71	149	111	3.0	2
Philippines	43	73	71	2.1	1
Thailand	42	75	77	2.3	1
South Korea	37	57	55	1.7	1
Egypt	37	65	77	2.3	1
Nigeria	63	135	114	3.0	2
Brazil	109	226	108	2.9	4
Mexico	60	131	119	3.1	2
United States	214	248	16	0.6	4
USSR	254	309	21	0.8	5
Japan	112	133	19	0.7	2
Eastern Europe	130	152	17	0.6	2
Western Europe	344	378	10	0.4	6

Source: *Global 2000 Technical Report*, Tables 2–10.

** The policy implications are clear. The Third World has to continue its efforts to restrict population growth. Optimistic projections should not give us a false sense of security. In immediate terms the effort to control population cannot be slackened. Population can be viewed as potential wealth; but this requires imaginative policies and determined implementation. In the present context a growing population is a liability.

✳ ✳ A growing population needs food; food is the most basic of human needs. The grim forecasts of global food shortage have also proved to be a case of crying wolf, and recent advances in agricultural technology give us reason to believe that, with adequate research and efficient management, hunger is avoidable. In many Third World countries the output per head has doubled between 1959–75. Since 1950 the global per capita grain production has gone up 24%. Countries in Asia and Latin America have either crossed the threshold or they are all set to do so. The situation in many parts of Africa, however, remains desperate.

Statistics do not always tell the whole truth. Despite the fact that global food production has marginally overtaken population increase, several problems still persist. As of now, 3 billion people have to be fed in the Third World; the number will rise to 5.4 billion by the year 2000. While there is enough food to go round and in the years to come the situation is likely to improve, those living in absolute poverty do not have the resources to buy enough food to meet their normal calorie and protein needs. In Asia and Latin America agricultural production has registered definite growth having increased from 3% to more than 5%, but malnutrition and hunger still remain major problems. Africa provides a depressing picture. In a large group of countries on this continent the average annual growth in farm production, which in the 1960s was 2.8%, has stopped at 1.4%. Although corn is the staple of approximately 40% of Africans, the hunting and herding economy of the past, which still attracts many, can support only 100–150 persons per square mile, and the population of these areas is rising.

✳ ✳ There are several reasons for the anomalous situation. The prices of basic inputs of modern agriculture – land, water, fertilizers, pesticides, seeds of high yielding cereals – are all going up. These are reflected in current higher prices of main food crops. It makes it all the more difficult for those in absolute poverty to buy enough food. The situation is not likely to improve in the near future. Irrigation is becoming increasingly expensive and difficult. According to one estimate 394 million hectares are suitable for irrigation, but only about one-sixth have actual irrigation facilities. Much agriculture thus remains dependent on rainfall. Too little or too much of it, or rains at the wrong time, can play havoc with harvest of the year. It can also cause floods, and few Third World countries have adequate resources for dependable flood control schemes. The situation is made more complex because agricultural produce is being diverted for conversion into sources of energy. These substitutes are expensive; but they still make a saving in the total energy bill. Added to this, the changing food habits of the affluent minority adversely affect food availability for the less favourably placed.

The policy implications are clear. More land has to be brought under food crops. According to one conservative estimate over 1,000 million hectares of unexploited land in the Third World can be brought under cultivation. It has been suggested that some 2,220 million hectare remain unexploited. An additional 205 million hectares will have to be brought under cultivation in the next two decades. The cost of agricultural inputs will have to be brought down through continuous research and cheaper alternatives will have to be found. Storage losses will have to be prevented. Food for survival and physical well-being must have priority over its diversion to satisfy the energy needs of the affluent. At the same time those living in absolute poverty will have to be given an opportunity to enhance their earning capacity so that they are not forced to cut down on the minimum food needs. The continuing battle for increasing food production to match population increase poses a major challenge to scientific laboratories and experimental farms; inputs for the support and furtherance of these endeavours will have to be increased, extension agencies strengthened and people taught methods of more efficient food utilization. These steps are, however, unlikely to succeed if they are not accompanied by necessary structural change and far-reaching land reforms. Most developing societies are dragging their feet in these areas. Food security is a critical and vulnerable area of development where the highest degree of self-reliance must be insisted upon. National self-respect and dignity are the first casualties when there is not enough food to go round. Global jaunts, with a begging bowl, for more food aid should not be a regular feature of the annual cycle of activities of Third World leaders.

The menacing energy crisis has sent shock waves through both the developed and the developing world. Even some of the highly industrialized countries became hysterical when the prices of petroleum were raised; the developing countries, of course, were the worst hit and in the interest of Third World solidarity they could not even protest. To focus attention exclusively on limited petroleum resources and its higher cost, however, is not the right way to assess the energy problem. Petroleum supplies only some 40% of the total world energy demand. There is no immediate danger of oil wells drying up; in fact new sources have been found in Mexico and elsewhere, and many countries like India have intensified their search for oil and achieved considerable success in these efforts. Despite rising cost, especially during the last decade, petroleum is still cheaper than most of its substitutes. Other energy sources are in short supply only relatively speaking; they can be exploited further, but at higher unit cost. The real energy problem lies elsewhere.

Energy use in the contemporary world is generally wasteful, uneconomic in the long run and in many instances not environmentally sound. Rising standards of living make exaggerated domestic demand on the available supplies of energy. Much of this can be drastically reduced; the Third World will have to contemplate determined measures in this direction. In industry cost-efficient energy use strategies will have to be adopted and wherever possible less energy-intensive techniques will have to be used. Domestic and industrial use of energy is so high that only a measly share is left for application to the agricultural sector. As of now only about 3.5% of the total world use of commercial energy goes into crop and livestock production; the share of the developing countries in 1972–73 was only 18% of the total world use. As mentioned earlier, fertilizer, pesticide, agricultural machinery, irrigation, food processing and food storage require greater energy inputs. If the projected target of agricultural growth rate of 3.7% is to be achieved, the use of commercial energy in the agricultural sector will have to rise about 8% and perhaps more in the 1980s and 1990s according to an FAO estimate. Food being the prime necessity of survival, agricultural production must have this share of energy use.

On the whole a second look at industrial technology is necessary to make it less energy-intensive. Cheaper forms of energy will have to be used in place of more expensive and scarce energy sources. In several sectors a return to coal may be necessary so that other, more costly fossil fuels can be used where they are needed more and in a cost-efficient manner. There is growing evidence of energy-cropping. For example, Brazil, US and the Philippines have stepped up sugarcane and corn production to obtain alternative energy sources for automobiles. In Brazil alone sugar-cane is being grown on over one million hectares of land exclusively for production of energy substitutes. It can be assumed that at least a part of it goes on luxury consumption and not on public utilities. Brazil, with its vast untapped land resources, can afford the land; many others cannot. Care will have to be taken to ensure that such a conversion does not adversely affect the already precarious food security of the Third World. New technologies can be found to obtain energy from crop wastes rather than from their edible parts.

There is no cause for alarm; new sources of energy can be found. But the greatest caution in conservation and economic energy utilization is necessary. Power can be derived from the sun, wind and waves. Geo-thermal energy also remains to be tapped. Some gains have been registered in the utilization of solar energy, but like atomic energy it continues to be costly. The technology for drawing energy from the wind and the waves has also made some progress, but their contribution to the total energy need is fractional. Research and development efforts will have to be accelerated in search of new sources of energy, especially for forms of energy from sources that have infinite capacity to yield them. Perhaps the most pressing problem is that of domestic fuel. There is an increasing tendency to use electricity and petrogas. This is both expensive and wasteful. Sewage gas is being developed in urban areas and for rural areas gas is being produced from biomass. These efforts are still in an experimental stage and their returns have not been very rewarding. Intensification of search in this field is indicated. New forestry programmes must be planned so that the countryside becomes self-sufficient for its domestic energy needs which consists, in many parts of the Third World, of wood fuel. China, the Republic of Korea, Thailand and some other countries have made successful experiments in this field. Many other Third World countries are taking up programmes of social forestry.

The challenge of the energy crisis can be met, but it will require tremendous human effort and substantial physical inputs. To be able to conserve, augment and supplement available energy sources institutional arrangements will have to be strengthened and even altered. Like food, energy programmes cannot wait; in fact the two are inextricably interlinked.

Developing Planning and Administrative Apparatus

A good policy can go wrong if the institutional mechanism to implement it is inadequate, inefficient or corrupt. The new paradigm of development contemplated here requires acceptance, not only at the level of emotional or intellectual awareness, but at the level where it affects the basic assumptions of planners as well as the administrative/implementing agencies.

The civil services, cast mostly in the colonial mould, have not truly accepted the philosophy of people's access to planning and participative development style, nor have they understood the different dimensions and ramifications of human resources mobilization. In fairness to them, however, it should be conceded that they had to subserve the power interests of difficult, mercurial and often immature political masters, to assume roles for which they were not trained and that they were constantly harassed by contrary pressures. Delivery systems have been enriched and under certain conditions they work efficiently; but the point to be noted is that the bureaucracy can work *for* the people but that it has some mental blocks when it comes to working *with* the people or *under* the people. This has to change. Even the delivery systems have to be streamlined in consonance with the new philosophy. The inadequacies of the bureaucratic structure at the middle and lower levels have emerged in clear relief and require substantial reorganization, training and retraining. Unless this is done the idea of grassroots planning (or planning from below) will never be attained and the access of the people to planning and development will continue to be denied.

Many Third World countries have excellently trained experts at the highest planning level. They know sophisticated techniques and econometrics. The only snag is that they incline either to the Western liberal model of planning or to the Soviet model, or in moments of desperation try blindly to copy the Chinese way of doing things. Endogenous creativity is not much in evidence. The most perfect econometric models fail to comprehend complex cultural reality and contextual specificities. The best and most logically consistent models of planning and development are not necessarily those that produce the best results. Fingers on the pulse of the people and responsiveness to their urges can impart to plans a sense of realism and relevance.

It has been noted that most plan documents are conceptually well formulated and well founded – if their premises are accepted. The top planners, however, leave the mundane and humdrum job of project formulation and project appraisal to those further down the bureaucratic hierarchy. This very often proves inadequate and defective. The methodologies of project evaluation, over the years, have become increasingly sophisticated, involving as they do technical performance comparisons, supporting forecasts, investment effectiveness studies, global economic cost evaluations, appraisal of environmental effects, technical and economic evaluations, technical–social cost–benefit ratings, multidisciplinary analyses of selected aspects, multi-impact evaluations and comprehensive assessments of all other relevant aspects. But these are restricted mostly to international agencies or to higher level national agencies working in the field of development cooperation. Some perceptive and insightful comments on the limits and possibilities of project assessment at these levels have been wittily made in the publication *Evaluating the Evaluation Game* by Aant Eliginza (1981), brought out as a SAREC Report.[2] It should be noted that some of these techniques are blindly applied to country situations without testing them for their relevance, reliability and validity. On the whole, project formulation and appraisal remains a vulnerable area often the Achilles heel of the planning endeavour in Third World countries. Inefficiently formulated projects, whose appraisal is also ineffective, result in the collapse of otherwise feasible plans. Monitoring and evaluation of projects on the ground needs strengthening so that desirable policy shifts may be made in time and costly failures avoided. Surveillance of short term and long term as well as intended and unintended consequences is necessary. Strengthening of these instrumentalities requires serious consideration and should be built into the policy process itself.

Communication links are often found to be weak and wide gaps persist between the planner, the implementation agencies and the people. There is a distortion of messages as they descend from the highest levels to the people at the bottom. The feedback is not properly organized; even when it is received its impact is minimal, unless the situation assumes critical proportions. Refashioning and reorganization of the communication network from top-down to bottom-up is necessary.

Management of Change

Governance, as mentioned earlier, is becoming increasingly arduous and hazardous. Violence is on the increase; individuals, groups and governments all contribute to it in different degrees. The sanctity of several institutions of society has eroded. There is little consensus on the goals of society; the moral quality of instrumentalities of action gets scant consideration. Many forms of corruption have been covertly legitimized. Statecraft has become amoral and cynical. Values have become diluted beyond recognition. The affluent countries are finding the task of management as difficult as their poorer cousins. The industrially advanced societies have to contend with the problems of recession, inflation, unemployment, as well as having to handle counter-currents of varying strength. The Third World countries find their predicament worse: in different degrees, directly or indirectly, they have to face all the problems confronting the industrially advanced countries, but have in addition also to meet the threat of the spectre of poverty. Mounting frustrations within lead to a search for desperate remedies and generate a great deal of senseless and destructive activity that can only be justified as an expression of helpless rage. Governments are responding to this discontent by increasingly resorting to Mafia methods.

The vexatious problems of governance have intra-national as well as international dimensions. Intra-nationally they emerge from lack of the promised development and its thin and uneven spread. The politics of poverty is essentially the politics of gaining control over limited and hard to obtain resources. It turns into a ceaseless and often mindless struggle in which it is hard to determine who is whose enemy. None the less, as the development process takes place, disparities are widened rather than reduced. This in itself causes tensions; but considered in conjunction with the egalitarian urge that has been assiduously kindled by the élite, it enhances the potential for conflict. The battle is really for access to and participation in decision-making. Closely linked to it is the strong desire for autonomy, which sets into motion mobilization mechanisms in which battle lines are drawn between ethnic and religious groups, minorities and majorities, regions, sexes, generations and dominant and counter-cultures. Misdirected modernization leads to a sense of freedom without parallel sense of responsibility, choice without faith and excessive concern for individual interest in total disregard of the collective interest. The examples set by the élite, especially a section of its leaders, are hardly noble and inspiring. There is as wide a gap between what they profess and what they practise as between their promise and performance. Their lifestyles are luxurious beyond decency. It should not surprise anyone, least of all the élite and the leadership, if they fail to inspire confidence. The politics of populism often becomes the politics of opportunism. There is a lack of vision in government leadership which fails to read the warning implicit in the developing trends, anticipate problems and act. Finally, the masses act in unpredictable and destructive ways because of lack of conscientization. They mistakenly feel that this is the only way they can be heard. The leadership likes to drive them like a flock of sheep; when it loses control the flock acts mindlessly. Conscientization is avoided for fear it will unmask the leadership so that people will see the truth.

International cross-currents contribute significantly to the upheavals within the Third World, which is unwittingly, caught up with the interests and conflicts of one or the other of the superpowers and their allies. As the history of the non-alignment movement proves, neutrality in superpower conflict has limited rewards and many penalties. Several Third World countries join these alliances, in the interest of their rulers and for limited and temporary gains. It is a case of accepting captivity by invitation. Those who refuse the carrots so temptingly dangled before them can anticipate an uncertain future which could range from engineered destabilization, to a coup, to assassination. Meanwhile the battle for minds goes on relentlessly. Ideologies are for export. Sometimes they are attractively but deceptively packaged. Everything, including subversion, is fair in the name of ideology and national interest. Several progressive regimes have been browbeaten by barely disguised blackmail and pressure; the most ruthless methods of extinction have been followed towards others. Surveillance by satellite leaves little that is secret at least to the superpowers and their principal allies. Espionage and counter-espionage by the CIA, KGB and their analogues is frequent. At no other time in the history of our cultural development has force been glamourized to the degree that it is today. In the final analysis all these activities result in maintenance of super-ordinate and subordinate relationships and are invariably used against movements for genuine liberation.

Alongside the pressures from great powers we have to take note of several transnational movements which add new complexities to the problems of governments. Humankind seems to be passing through the era of searching for great causes, and of revolutionary activity toward their realization. Causes abound, and so do the revolutions associated with them. These transnational movements may have religious and spiritual overtones or they may be frankly revolutionary political ideologies; in either case they have unsettling effects. The export of religious/spiritual cults from East to the West – Mahesh Yogi and his TM, Anand Marg and its PROUT, the Hare Krishna movement, Rajneesh and his special brand of spiritualism, Zen and several other recipes for instant nirvana – cannot be written off as bizarre happenings of no or little consequence in the receiving countries. From minor irritants, some of them are becoming quite serious problems. Several brands of Islamic ideology, from fundamentalism to Islamic Marxism, are also for export. Without commenting on their merit or otherwise we can anticipate the social consequences. A resurgence of fundamentalist or revolutionary Islam in a country like India, which has the world's third largest Muslim population and is slowly settling down to cultural pluralism within a composite framework and adjusting to a secular and democratic polity, could be unsettling and unpredictable. As for revolutionary ideologies, there is a rich spread to choose from. They represent a dimension of the contemporary reality which is little understood but which nevertheless adds to the problems that governments have to face both in the developed and the developing worlds.

The international order is chaotic and getting worse. The basic malady is unequal control over resources, i.e. unequal distribution of power. Too few control too much of the total resource supplies of the world. Unless their distribution is organized on a logical and just basis the world will continue to remain in turmoil. In the past three decades the more industrialized countries have thrown some crumbs by way of aid to the Third World. This has been woefully inadequate; a form of charity in which the giver knew best what was good for the beneficiary. Even this charity came in driblets. It temporarily stabilized some regimes, but failed to produce any real development. The Third World today is rightly wary of such charitable aid. Articulate groups of analysts have shown clearly that the industrial affluence of much of the West has been built mainly on ruthless exploitation of the resources of the Third World. Transfer of resources is demanded as compensation, if not as a reparation.

This argument has truth behind it, but it cannot be pressed beyond a point. How can the affluent and the powerful be persuaded to make amends for the exploitative deeds of their progenitors? It would be more logical to argue for transfer of resources in the interest of a stable world order. Sizable transfer of resources is a survival imperative – but how are we to achieve this? Aid and trade have been the subject of endless argument in which much rhetoric has been wasted. Confrontation has produced much heat but little light. Dialogue has to continue; but it has also to be followed up by action. In the meanwhile the industrially advanced countries are staking more and more claims to common global resources – resources in the seas and the resources in the Antarctic. If they had their way the superpowers would perhaps divide even outer space among themselves. When it comes to sharing of resources or paying even fair prices for the produce of the Third World, affluent countries innocently plead that their economies are in bad shape, that they have recession, inflation and unemployment. The Third World recognizes the prevalence of these problems but analyses their causes differently. The developed world continues to make massive financial outlays for staggering armaments build-up, but drags its feet when it comes to transfer of resources for global development for the benefit of those living in absolute poverty. The gap between the developing and the developed is widening in respect of economic strength and military power, science and technology and general standards of living.

North–South dialogue and confrontation have both proved sterile. An equitable and just pattern of interdependence is nowhere in sight. The Third World has no collective muscle, despite a facade of unity and talk about the Arusha spirit, the Nairobi spirit, the Cancun spirit and, most recently, the Delhi spirit. It remains disunited. This lack of unity is taken advantage of by the affluent and the powerful nations. Because of the lack of their capacity for collective action much Third World rhetoric goes to waste. The oil example humbled the mighty up to a point, but it is as yet unclear how this example can be followed by other commodities exported by the Third World. The Third World will have to learn to resolve its differences and resist the blandishments of the superpowers who are only too willing to part with the toys of destruction so that the Third World may be preoccupied with war games. Schemes of national self-sufficiency and intra-Third World cooperation will have to be strengthened. A series of Third World institutions and a global network of institutions, with First and Second World participation, aimed at genuine development, will have to be set up. Humble beginnings have been made by the United Nations University in limited spheres. At the same time, non-emulative paths of development which encourage orthogenetic growth and endogenous creativity have to be found and strengthened. Alternative styles of life most suited and relevant to Third World conditions have to be legitimized.

In an uncharted area like the management of change no definitive answers can be given. They have to be found by trial and error and one of the policy imperatives is that the search must be initiated and sustained.

Notes

1. Matthews, William H., "The Concept of Outer Limits", in William H. Matthews (ed.), *Outer Limits and Human Needs*, Uppsala, Dag Hammarskjöld Foundation, 1976.

2. Elzinga, Aant, *Evaluating the Evaluation Game: On the Methodology of Project Evaluation, with Special Reference to Development Cooperation*, Stockholm, Swedish Agency for Research Cooperation with Developing Countries, 1981.

6　Framework of Action

Assuming that true development involves investment in people to enable them and society first to meet their basic needs and then gradually to improve their quality of life, a framework of action consisting of conscientization, affirmative action, and institution building is presented here. The guidelines to action implicit in this framework are no easy do-it-yourself manual, nor are any cookbook recipes offered. The action implications are complex but necessary. This is no utopia; it is an agenda for reflection and action.

Conscientization is to be viewed as an instrument of liberation and responsibility. It is conceded that its immediate consequences may be somewhat disconcerting to the prevailing power structure; but it cannot be denied that in the final analysis it would enhance human self-esteem, impart a high degree of sense of social responsibility and ultimately prove to be an effective tool of human resources enrichment and mobilization. Affirmative action, on the other hand, constitutes social action to rectify past injustices with a view to allowing specially deprived and degraded groups to rise from their present sub-human standards to acceptable human standards. Institution building emphasizes people's access to and participation in the great adventure of development. The modernization process operates through a series of complex organizations; renovation and innovation in these are imperative. In sum, the strategy projected is one of making essential inputs into restoring human dignity to people, into making them reflective and active members of society and into restructuring some basic institutions to enhance their performance capability.

Conscientization

The relationship between power and development, despite three decades of passionately argued theoretical positions and painstaking research conducted with a sense of urgency, continues to be a grey area, marked either by a tendency to skirt around gut issues by unquestioningly accepting the views of the national élites or optimistic assumptions that the ramifications of the programmes of action will, in time, bend the power structure in favour of those whose development needs are the greatest. We do not have to search wide and deep to discover the critical linkages between power on the one hand and choice of technology, income distribution, extension of welfare services and dynamics of decision-making on the other. All governments speak and, outwardly at least, claim to function in the name of the people and work for their benefit, but experience suggests that policy formulation and implementation are both weighted in favour of the ruling élite of the society. The loud and vociferous sections, having a developed expressive capability, are also beneficiaries in the sense that as a sop some gains of development are conceded to them. The masses in whose name all political manifestoes are prepared and whose betterment, apparently at least, is the credo of all political platforms – continue to stand somewhere towards the tail end of the queue and titbits are thrown to them as a gesture of generosity.

It is evident that the volume of absolute poverty has registered no significant decline in the low income countries of the world, especially in the Asian and Pacific region. The situation is as bad in Latin America, perhaps worse in Africa. According to reliable and widely accepted estimates, the number of people living in absolute poverty stands at around 800 million; some three-fourths of them are to be found in the rural areas and urban slums of Asia. They are the dispossessed and the degraded for whom the development process has held out many tantalizing hopes, of which none have materialized. Ambitious blueprints for their welfare are made, but they themselves have little say in determining their contents. Voiceless and perplexed, they watch the show conducted in their name; the élites determine their needs as well as the strategies of fulfilling them.

Endemic and absolute poverty breeds a culture of its own, that functions as a satellite to the culture of the dominant minority and whose *raison d'être* is to contribute, at bare survival wages, to the comforts and luxuries of the established and the emerging élite. The *World Development Report 1980* offers little satisfaction when it says that

> the proportion of the people in absolute poverty in developing countries as a group is estimated to have fallen during the past two decades... But because population has grown, the number of people in absolute poverty has increased.[1]

The prognosis contained in the earlier *World Development Report 1978* appears to hold true. To quote from it, "given the obstacles they face, elimination of absolute poverty in the low income countries by the end of the century seems impossible".[2] If the prevailing trends are any indication, the situation may continue well till the middle of the next century and even beyond. The rhetoric of egalitarianism and socialism notwithstanding, the masses continue to remain on the periphery of decision-making. Despite tiresome professions of democracy, only compliance is expected from the majority. Even in countries which have dismantled the exploitative class structure, it is open to question how much the people can articulate themselves and obtain a decisive say in making critical choices governing their future.

A frail little man – Paulo Freire – was moved by the plight of the underdog in Latin America. The masses here had come to accept misery and suffering as their lot and found themselves unable to do anything about their deprivation and degradation. He reflected on the human condition, focused specially on the Latin American poor, and assigned to education a new function – conscientization, which is the central focus of his book – *Pedagogy of the Oppressed*.[3] The function of education, as envisioned by him, is to conscientize the individual, the group and the community by enlarging their cognitive map and by imparting a critical awareness of their condition and the causes underlying it. He made a few small experiments in his revolutionary new pedagogy, which were found too inconvenient by the countries in which these trials were conducted. It was one thing to admire a brave and radical intellectual posture from a distance, quite another to permit the emergence and establishment of a pedagogy that would "subvert" the minds and threaten the power balance in the society. Freire was found to be a *persona non grata* in one country after another and had constantly to be on the move to find a more hospitable environment in which his ideas could be experimented upon. Operating from his headquarters in the traditionally neutral Switzerland, Freire looked for hosts who would dare go beyond admiring his innovative ideas and would let him carry out his experiments irrespective of the consequences they produced.

Despite its undoubted awkwardness the ubiquitous term conscientization has come to stay; this seminal notion has since been further refined and extended. There are many who believe that in the ultimate analysis it holds the key to genuine mass-oriented development.

Culture of Poverty

Before explicating the concept of conscientization, a brief detour towards understanding the culture of poverty will be in order. Misconceptions about its causes and consequences have led to a great deal of erring and ill conceived development. After all, it is the poor at whom much of the development activity is focused and it is essential to see if their special cultural predicament has any elements which hinder or inhibit absorption of the elements of change that are considered essential for improvement to their quality of life.

For a long time the behavioural sciences appeared to pretend in their analyses that rich/poor differences, although they existed, mattered little. The development process, as prescribed and generally accepted, was bound to reduce the gap. A degree of inequality was natural; only its harshness needed rectification. It was left to Oscar Lewis to study in depth the substratum of the urban poor and the cultural implications of poverty in Latin America.[4] His vivid and dramatic portrayals of individuals and families from the poverty substratum demonstrate with great effect how poverty demeans and dehumanizes a sizable section of humanity. The locale of Lewis' studies were mostly urban slums which coexist alongside the elegant towers of prosperity in different countries of Latin America; but his concept of the culture of poverty has much wider implications and can be used, partially at least, in understanding the nature of poverty and its consequences elsewhere. He elaborates his methodology at fair length and uses bold strokes of his brush to paint the profiles of the poor studied by him.

Drawing from the voluminous work of Oscar Lewis (especially 1966) and its several critiques, treatment of the theme by others and broadly following Leeds (1971), we can chart the traits that are characteristic of the culture of poverty.[5]

Some features are nearly universal in poverty cultures: life expectancy is relatively low; death rates are high; the proportion of younger age group is higher; as both children and women work, the proportion of those having some kind of employment is also higher; the world view is provincially and locally oriented; this sector is at best only partially integrated into the network of national institutions; levels of literacy and education are low; they are neither organized into unions nor are they members of political parties; social security schemes such as medical care, maternity, or other benefits do not exist for them; and they make little use of the cities' hospitals, department stores, museums and galleries.

Examining these traits in a global perspective some modifications are indicated. The children and women forming part of the workforce do so under the compulsion of economic necessity; they are given menial, tedious and repetitive chores, and are almost always underpaid. The low levels of literacy and education are explained by the non-functional nature of the education imparted, poor educational facilities and ineffective enforcement of compulsory education provisions where they exist. The urban poor, and to a lesser extent the rural poor also, are becoming unionized; but the multiplicity of unions, each exercising a contrary pull, makes them ineffective. Lacking a broad vision, most such unions strive to gain only some petty and short-range objectives. Political parties need the poor as vote banks and before each national election considerable solicitude is lavished on them. They are seduced by populist slogans and revolutionary rhetoric, but once the election is over they continue to suffer benign neglect. What is important is that they invariably cannot reach the decision-making echelons of the parties and cannot assert themselves enough to effect meaningful changes in their manifestoes. This denial of access to planning results in lopsided priorities and unwanted and irrelevant reforms. Social security measures are being introduced and social services are being extended, both ostensibly for the poor. The poor do wish to take advantage of them; but what is offered is so indifferent in quality and so difficult and cumbersome to obtain that the poor tend to rely on their own devices, however deficient they be.

Let us return to the Lewis formulation and list the economic traits presented by him. These include: constant struggle for survival; unemployment and underemployment; low wages for unskilled occupations; child labour; absence of savings, chronic shortage of cash; absence of food reserves in the home, resulting in frequent buying of small quantities of food as need arises; pawning and borrowing from local moneylenders at exorbitant rate of interest; spontaneous informal credit devices organized by neighbours; and the use of secondhand clothing and furniture. These traits are nearly universal, with only minor regional and cultural variations.

Some social and psychological attributes, Lewis suggests, become characteristic of the culture of poverty. Of necessity the people have to live in crowded quarters. Its consequences are twofold: while there is general lack of privacy, gregariousness increases. There is high incidence of alcoholism and frequent resort to violence in settling quarrels, training children and getting the wife to obey the wishes of the husband. Sexual initiation takes place early in life and breaches of norms in respect of matrimonial alliances is condoned with relative ease. The marital bond is fragile; desertion and divorce are common. There is a relatively high incidence of abandonment of mothers and children. The general trend is towards mother-centred families and greater proximity to maternal relatives. There is great emphasis on family solidarity with the nuclear family predominating. In general the family structure is authoritarian, though mechanisms exist for the easy solution of dissent and deviance.

These traits may be true in respect of the Latin American urban poor; but they cannot be universalized. Some of them characterize, in varying degrees, the culture of poverty elsewhere; but other cultural contexts and deep-seated traditions significantly alter them.

Finally, let us look at some of the other traits forming part of the Lewis inventory. People in the culture of poverty have a strong orientation to the here and now, inability to defer gratification and to plan for the future, a sense of resignation and fatalism based upon the realities of a difficult life situation, a belief in male superiority, a martyr complex among women, and high tolerance for psychological pathology of all sorts. Further, those living in a culture of poverty have a critical attitude towards some of the values and institutions of the dominant class. There is a mistrust of government and those in high positions and cynicism extends even to religious institutions and secular services such as education and medicare. From the later work of Lewis, we get an additional trait list. This includes a strong feeling of marginality; helplessness; not belonging; alienation; feeling that existing institutions do not serve their interests and needs; feelings of powerlessness; inferiority; personal unworthiness; very little sense of history; constricted vision, involving knowledge only of their local and neighbourhood conditions and their own way of life; and little knowledge, vision, or ideology to see similarities with their counterparts elsewhere in the world; absence of class consciousness; and a sensitivity to status distinction. These traits appear to be nearly universal in poverty cultures in all parts of the world; their expression, however, differs in different cultural universes.

Excellent as Lewis' analytic ethnography is, it fails to explain why the poor are poor and are likely to remain so. His analyses are ahistorical and do not examine the emergence of exploitative and oppressive structures that have resulted in mass poverty and sub-human standards of living. He also fails to explain the tyrannical nature of the authority which does not permit the poor to raise their standards appreciably. Nowhere does it emerge in his writing that poverty is not a self-inflicted torture which cannot be attributed to any of the innate deficiencies of the poor. The vicious circle can be broken; but Lewis has no concrete suggestions as to how. He stops short of suggesting how the structures of oppression and tyranny can be dismantled and the poor can find a new life for themselves. He does not even hint that this could be done by conscientization and mass mobilization. In sum, what we get from him are a series of impressive and deeply moving profiles; but diagnostically and prognostically his work does not offer any significant leads to action.

What is Conscientization
Conscientization may be understood as a process of cognitive and evaluative transformation, especially in the poor of the world. It enables the individual to contemplate the environment and the human condition and gain an understanding of the forces that are shaping the contemporary world. Of special interest is the interplay of social, economic, and political currents that result in inequities and injustices in the social order. The individual begins to ask: Why? How? What Next?

Such reflective exercises, hopefully, will bring home the realization that deprivation and misery are not god-given, nor are they the result of any innate deficiencies in the poor as a group. By and by the poor would begin to analyse the structures of exploitation and oppression that have brought vast sections of humanity to their present predicament.

Conscientized people would not resign themselves to their fate, accepting their lot as inevitable and irreversible. With a developed sense of history and critical awareness of the issues and intricacies in the working of the present social order, they will develop the faith that human intervention can alter the situation and the processes of history can be accelerated. They would persuade themselves to believe that alternatives that would take them towards a preferred future and new designs for living are available.

They would also know that social disparities can neither be wished away nor eradicated by a simple movement of some magic wand. With their awakened understanding of societal processes and their inner dynamics, they would distrust all instant panaceas. They would critically assess the promises and performance of those in power and those aspiring to attain it. Thus, political parties would not be able to take them for granted. A conscious citizenry would be the best guarantee for the success of a participative democracy, by whatever political label it went.

Those without a share, or voice, in vital decision-making processes will begin to assert and express themselves, with a degree of bluntness and even ruthlessness where it is indicated. They will have gradually conceptualized the kind of future they wish to build for themselves and will have concretized, in a broad outline, the strategy (including steps and stages) by which the desired goals can be achieved.

In the final analysis, conscientization would produce autonomous individuals who would understand, accept and respect their linkages with a wider society – national and international. They would be reflective individuals, who would at the same time have a participative nature and a positive action orientation. They would be capable of making responsible choices and have the inner strength and self-discipline to pursue them resolutely. They would be *homo faber* in the true sense. To the extent that meaningful intervention in the processes of policy formulation and implementation is essential, they would be politicized. In consequence, the content and quality of politics would undergo changes, for their new psychological disposition would be bound to demand them.

Education for liberation, thus, would have to incorporate elements of conscientization. A dose of conscientization is indicated also for the affluent and the more fortunate. Their continued insensitivity to the plight of the masses can throw the social order off balance; in the resultant convulsions they may lose a great deal. Adaptation to the emerging reality may be a less painful option.

Achieving Conscientization
We could perhaps refine the concept of conscientization further and produce a more elegant and sophisticated formulation; but such an exercise can wait, for elegance and sophistication do not necessarily add to the feasibility and operational facility of a concept. The answer to the question "How to bring about conscientization?" is elusive and difficult. The institutions and instrumentalities that could make a valuable contribution to the process are controlled by interests that are antithetical, or at any rate not favourably disposed, towards improving the lot of the poor and the downtrodden. They may be scared by the possible implications and ramifications of an imaginative conscientization programme and choose to keep away from it.

The school system is geared to the maintenance of status quo. As Ivan Illich (1971) has poignantly pointed out, the schooling process is aimed at producing a product that is packaged for the consumer society and at fitting into predetermined slots – roles and statuses – in the social order.[6] Such a process can hardly be conducive to the promotion of non-consumerism and to fundamental changes in the social order. What is worse, far from having a pedagogy for conscientization we still do not have an effective pedagogy for first generation learners to cover their normal school subjects. Some radical pedagogic departures are indicated. In this field, however, the question is whether the powers that be will permit their emergence?

The mass media have belied the hopes and expectations placed in them regarding educational policies and objectives. The cinema and TV have turned into instruments of escapist entertainment rather than of genuine mass education. When the other media are also controlled by commercial interests it is only natural that they should serve the interests of their masters; when state-controlled they function as apologists and mouthpieces of those occupying seats of power. It may be added that the question of their effective utilization is largely hypothetical for insofar as the poor are concerned the media are class rather than mass media. The same holds true of the newspapers also. The controlling interests determine their policy guidelines. In the prevailing state of mass illiteracy, however, for the time being at least, they are irrelevant as their mass impact is bound to be low. By slow stages a new turn can be given to the communication policies of the low income countries; but it is doubtful that this will produce a great leap forward towards genuine conscientization in the short run.

Political parties and organized unions have a definite and positive role, although even their performance has not so far been impressive. It appears to be ridden with ambiguities and contradictions. Concern for poverty has become the signature tune of all political parties in most countries of the Third World, but the populist postures and promises are often no more than political gimmicks. Unionized interests either enter into unholy alliances with the dominant power in society or begin to reflect a narrow sectional interest. Some of these organized interests have done reasonably well by themselves; but in doing so they have zealously prevented the spread of benefits to those less fortunate.

A powerful case can be made out that in the larger and long-range interest of society governmental intervention in favour of conscientization is desirable and necessary. Thinking and conscious individuals will be more amenable to accepting a disciplined approach to social objectives and the instrumentalities for attaining them. In the long run this would make governance – a task which is becoming increasingly difficult with every passing year – easier. If and when this happens, a new sense of direction can be given to the state-run educational and media systems to reorient their offerings. But moves in this direction are bound to be slow, unsure and hesitant. Most governments prefer the soft options of pragmatism to hard choices for a meaningful and sustainable future. With their myopia they are likely to see the negative aspects of conscientization and ignore its positive potential. Initially it is bound to be somewhat unsettling – but only temporarily. The long-range pay-off is what matters and this would certainly be rewarding. If the intentions regarding a new social order are honest, conscientization is imperative; Third World governments must recognize it.

The need for voluntary action, possibly the most potent instrument of conscientization, would still remain. The magnitude of the task is so immense that it calls for a massive mobilization effort. Mercifully, reserves of altruism still survive and it is not impossible to find enthusiastic workers motivated by a service ethic. Their latent energies have to be identified, organized and galvanized into purposeful action. Initiatives in this field will have to be carefully planned.

The situation today is infinitely complex and appears to defy all solution. But the conspiracy of silence regarding the nature and causes of poverty and

of possible ways of eradicating them will have to be broken. Conscientization is the one way out; but its operational mechanics are not easy to
determine.

✳ Another Education(A)

The emphasis on conscientization should not be misconstrued as a denigra-
tion of formal education. Education is both an instrument and an indicator
of development. It may not be a sufficient condition for development but it
is none the less necessary. The infinite range of tasks implicit in the development process call for trained competence and expertise in wide and
varying fields. As such, excellence in education is to be sought; in fact it has
to be promoted with an unrelenting zeal.

But it is necessary at the same time to keep in mind the spread, nature
and social consequences of education. The present system is highly restric-
tive and its benefits naturally go more to the privileged segments of society.
The poor and the underprivileged either have no education at all or at best
they have only notional education. Some groups from these sections do
consciously seek opportunities for education; but their motivation is rarely
oriented toward a genuine learning ethic. To most of them education is
either a status symbol or means of upward mobility. Those just above the
bottom 40% find education useful also for dealing with new situations such
as interaction with administrative and developmental bureaucracy or the
timing and precision called for by modern agricultural methods. The bottom
stratum of the society, by and large, remains indifferent to it for education
has no remedies to offer for their immediate existential problems and its
content does not relate to the vital contexts of their lives. Education can do
little to break the conspiracy of social factors and forces that make upward
mobility an unrealizable dream for them.

In thinking about another development we also simultaneously have to
think about another education. Consideration of alternatives in development presupposes the consideration of alternatives in education.

Contrary to the claims made about education as a great equalizer and
mobility multiplier, it has been found that it contributes to the maintenance
of an unequal pattern of stratification prevailing in society. The educated
emerge in certain contexts as the most determined and cruel defenders of
their class interests and privileges. It is well known also that education leads
to an artificial and socially detrimental distinction between manual and
mental labour. Insofar as the poor are concerned education has an alienat-
ing effect. It uproots the recipients from their traditional moorings; they
begin to seek or develop new identities. This may possibly be good for the
individuals concerned; but the community in general is bound to be critical
for little benefit accrues to it. The alternative educational system must
ensure that its products retain organic links with their community. The
really poor find education a purposeless luxury for it involves loss of the
earnings of school-age children, however meagre they may be.

The ideas of equity and social justice justify another education which would radically alter the present pattern in favour of the deprived and the degraded. A major component of the new educational policies would be affirmative action – or positive discrimination – in favour of those who have so far been denied the advantages of education. To make education effective a series of pedagogic innovations would be necessary. Underplaying the tendency to emphasize academic learning, education will have to be related to living concerns and vital life contexts of the people. The present system is highly competitive; the new system would have to be non-competitive and would have to be built around cooperation. Similarly, the new system should not be individual-centred; it must be interactional and group-oriented. It would permit free play of expression and creativity to both individuals and collectivities of different kinds. In it the emphasis throughout would be on sharpening problem-solving capabilities. It would incorporate desirable values for a new social order, especially a new work and distributional ethic. It would equip learners to contemplate their environments and find remedies for persisting imbalances and injustices. If the new pedagogy is tailored to this objective, we can expect the emergence of a true learning ethic in society.

This is one aspect of the problem; massive illiteracy is another. It is estimated that some one billion people in the world are illiterate; 900 million among them live in the Third World. As an aside it may be added that about 100 million persons in the United States and Europe are also functionally illiterate; but their presence is no consolation to the Third World. What accounts for this depressing state of affairs? Low financial outlays? Poor teaching? Irrelevance of the offerings? Lack of commitment? Or, perhaps all of these and more? With the exception of China, adult education programmes have proved to be expensive misadventures. It appears that the Third World leadership has some hidden fears about social upheavals that mass education may bring about, although they cannot articulate them openly. Such lurking doubts, if they exist, are symptoms of a myopic vision. Prevalence of illiteracy will befuddle and obstruct the development process, and also lead to a general weakening of the normative structure; weak norms and their poor enforcement result in social disorder. In these societies politicization without conscientization can be disaster. Conscientization and education should be the two sides of the same coin. One cannot be separated from the other and unless the two are simultaneously geared to the attainment of the objective of development progress with justice will continue to elude us.

Affirmative Action

One of the major dilemmas of development, and of modernization, is that its benefits are unevenly distributed: the advantaged tend to get more advantaged and the disadvantaged become more so. The experience of the last three decades has been that while the general volume of poverty has increased, some of the rich have become super-rich. The stratum in between has also derived some benefits; but these are more in the nature of a few symbols of better life and do not offer them genuine and dependable security. The experience of most Third World countries has been that a large part of the gains of development have been cornered by the powerful and the influential; the neediest have had to be content with only notional benefits. This is so because the economic, social and political institutions are weighted in favour of the thin upper crust of society. The persisting imbalance results in loss of faith in the development process for the majority. Frustrations mount and tensions build up.

Equality of economic opportunity viewed as free competition perpetuates the status quo, if it does not actually tip the balance further to the advantage of the haves as against the have-nots. Because of the prevailing disparities the concept of one man, one vote is reduced to a ritual. It only gives the semblance of power to the people; the substance is held back from them. They can dislodge one government and instal another in its place, but in this process the class character and interest of the government do not undergo a significant change. At the societal level patterns of stratification continue to persist: inequity and injustice remain the lot of the masses. The poorest among the poor fare the worst in the process; currents of progress pass them by without, in any significant measure, alleviating their misery and sufferings. It is for the more wretched among the wretched of the earth that a policy of affirmative action – positive discrimination – has been recommended and adopted in varying degrees by several countries.

Target Groups

While the main thrust of the development programmes in most Third World countries is on poverty eradication generally, and must remain so, some special cases call for special attention. Their sub-human standards require immediate remedial measures and fast rectification. These cases are certain social categories that have been the victims of extreme cultural deprivation and continue to suffer centuries-old discrimination in the economic, social, and political spheres. In addition to their general economic backwardness, several such groups have to suffer social stigmas of one kind or another. Even in the superdeveloped countries like the United States of America, Blacks are not only economically disadvantaged, they also have to suffer a series of social indignities. The position of American Indians and migrants of Latin origin is only slightly better. In India untouchability has been abolished by law, although this legislative fiat has not materially altered the socially degraded status of its victims. Women now recognize the baneful effects of gender discrimination and are keen to redress their sex-linked inferiority.

Positive discrimination has been practised in the USA towards Blacks, American Indians and Spanish-speaking minorities who have migrated to the north from Central and South America. All these groups suffer some special disadvantages and pose problems which are not rooted in poverty

(cont.)
alone. On the other hand India – a low income country – has several social categories which are economically disadvantaged as well as socially stigmatized: the former untouchables, the scheduled tribes or aborigines and certain backward classes. In Malaysia, the Orang Asli pose problems that are common to aborigines in many parts of the world, but a glaring problem is presented by the original Malay population – the Bumiputra – who, although they constitute a thin numerical majority, have not been able to keep pace economically with the Chinese, the largest ethnic and cultural minority, and are afraid of losing the battle for tertiary education, and therefore the opportunity of reaching the higher levels in the professions, both to the Chinese and the Indian sections of the population. While poverty figures among all the three ethnic groups, and is being attended to, a policy of positive discrimination is followed in favour of the Bumiputra so that they are prepared and equipped to compete on a basis of equality with the other ethnic groups. Wherever the philosophy of positive discrimination is accepted the targets are ethnic and cultural groups of certain identifiable social categories.

The case for positive discrimination in favour of women is different as it involves nearly one-half of humanity. In recent years it has been articulated with considerable force, especially in the International Year of Women, to focus attention on the question of sexual discrimination and culturally determined deprivation of women. From the point of view of equity and distribution women should participate equally in the process of development and have an equal share in its benefits. As development thinking has come to regard human beings as the central resources for affecting social change, women have equal right and responsibility to participate with men as agents of social transformation. The accent now is on human development; culturally drawn and sustained barriers cannot hold them from realizing their full potential.

What is Affirmative Action?
In the earlier thinking on the subject, affirmative action was viewed mainly as a preparatory step. It involved seeking out and preparing for better jobs individuals belonging to groups who were victims of age-old discriminatory prejudices. Over the years the thinking has changed as preparatory discrimination failed to produce the results expected from it. Now affirmative action appears to have acquired four identifiable but interrelated dimensions: protective, ameliorative, compensatory and participative. State protection, through legal enactment and enforcement, is considered necessary for these weak and vulnerable sections. One point of view even suggests that traditional judicial restraint should yield to judicial activism in support of the cause of these sections. The ameliorative dimensions requires that specially earmarked financial outlays, on a generous scale, should be made for the welfare and development of the target groups. The compensatory aspect implies privileged access to education, employment and housing. The underlying idea is that they should acquire statistical parity in educational

opportunities as well as in jobs and promotions. The tendency towards housing segregation should be overcome. Through state intervention and institutional restructuring people from these groups should be enabled to become equal in as short a period of time as possible. The participative dimension aims at their increased access to political power through reservations for membership in decision-making institutions at different levels. Things will not begin to happen unless the programme of affirmative action is informed by a dynamic vision of equity and justice and is implemented with a high degree of determination and resoluteness. The most discriminated against from the bottom 40% logically need to be considered first.

Issues in the Controversy

There is no dispute about the desirability of certain measure of affirmative action to help the specially deprived; but the criteria for the selection of the target groups as well as the nature and degree of positive discrimination are the subject of a hot debate. Should the criteria of inclusion follow ethnic and gender considerations? Should entire social categories consisting both of advantaged as well as less advantaged and definitely disadvantaged elements be included? Or should positive discrimination choose the target individuals and groups according to well formulated indicators of economic and social deprivation?

An acrimonious and strident controversy is raging on the question of affirmative action. The implementation of policies emanating from this principle have led to long-drawn legal battles in some countries. Several countries have experienced considerable social disquiet over the issue; some have had even minor convulsions. A potential threat is recognized in many others. Where fundamental changes in the foundations and fabric of society are intended the passage of reforms can rarely be smooth. None the less, vital questions cannot be shelved indefinitely for their long-range consequences can be more dangerous.

The case for affirmative action is made on several justifiable grounds. First, it is intended to rectify the injustices of the past. What several groups endured for many centuries cannot be prolonged any further in the new social ethos. It is unjust and immoral and any efforts to perpetuate it are likely to lead to severe upheavals. It is essential, therefore to begin with these deprived and discriminated groups and ensure economic and social justice for them. Second, it provides a realistic base for the upward mobility of deprived groups. It would naturally reduce the existing gap between different classes and categories of the population and pave the way for an egalitarian society. Third, without strong measures of affirmative action a framework for equity and justice cannot be evolved. Doles and charities are unproductive; they cannot solve the problems of long continued injustice. Only through affirmative action can a society rebuild itself from the foundations upwards so that the most deprived begin to realize their human worth and potential. Finally, such a policy would result in the emergence of a participative society, with a share in decision-making powers extended to those who have so far been denied them. Such a policy alone can lead to genuine national integration and to the equal participation of all sections in the development process.

The critics of affirmative action are vocal and assertive. They are of the view that such a policy would adversely affect equality of opportunity. It also contravenes the provisions of a normal democratic constitution, if the country has any. In certain situations, it can go against the fundamental rights of citizens whose claims may be passed over in the name of positive discrimination. This policy emphasizes equity, but in doing so it underplays merit. In consequence, the quality of education and public services are likely to suffer. Nations cannot be built on equity alone; merit, talent and excellence also have a powerful role. These are likely to be eroded if the notion of positive discrimination is carried beyond a certain point. Further, it is argued that affirmative action may result in the creation of permanent vested interests and these would be detrimental to the objectives of national integration. It is well known that some Blacks who could have passed as Whites in the USA now insist on recognition of their Black ethnic identity. American Indians now reiterate their Indianness. Discarded Spanish names are sought out once again and this ethnic–linguistic profile is ethusiastically projected. All this happens, it is said, because of the additional benefits that come to these groups from the policy of positive discrimination. The Indian experience also suggests that some groups develop a vested interest in backwardness and their new status because of all the benefits that they bring to them. This leads, in a way, to parasitism. The element of truth in these arguments cannot be denied; but they do not entirely demolish the case for positive action. At best they suggest caution and the need for an appropriate strategy to ensure that gap-reducing measures do not unintentionally increase social distinctions and contribute to strengthening of the great divide.

Comment

In conclusion, the case for affirmative action retains its validity although policies geared to it have to be implemented with care, caution and determination. It is a necessary but only a transitional phase in the development of a society. It is not intended to be a permanent feature. Fundamental rights and democratic norms cannot ignore the claims of equity and justice. No constitution is sacrosanct; it always has to be sensitive and responsive to the changing ethos and to the new urges articulated by large sections of the society. In a sense good intentions are always constitutional. What is necessary is to emphasize the preparatory aspects of affirmative action and carry out a meaningful policy of ameliorative and compensatory discrimination for a stipulated period. The basic objective is to prepare the weakest sections for equal participation, but before they can do so to afford them a measure of protection, amelioration and compensation. Given thoughtful planning and its careful implementation all this can be achieved in a few decades. In the beginning it will be necessary to include deprived ethnic groups and social categories as a whole for protection as well as development;

but gradually those achieving the requisite level of development will have to be excluded. For this a set of well defined indicators would be necessary. The programme should be aimed at ensuring that the hitherto deprived groups attain such levels of development as to make affirmative action redundant. This, of course, is a challenge to social action. Despite its hazards, there appears no viable alternative to affirmative action in the present context.

Institution Building

A feature of modern government that arrests attention is its excessive concentration of power and functions. The sphere of state activity has enlarged considerably; new responsibilities are added with every passing decade. There is a visible tendency on the part of governments to voluntarily assume increasing burdens and to arrogate to themselves more and more tasks that were earlier performed by other institutions and agencies. As a result there is a proliferation of ministries and departments; an already oversized bureaucracy continues to swell still further. A parallel trend is towards over-bureaucratization. The public services, modelled largely on the colonial pattern, have an ethos of their own. Their functioning is characterized by Red tape and bureaucratic formalism; there is a rigid insistence on following out dated rules and regulations and the bureaucracy finds itself unable to act where precedents do not exist. The efforts to bring about changes in post-colonial bureaucracy's operating culture have not produced the desired results; the change has been minimal and mostly superficial. It remains aloof and rigid and has not demonstrated a capacity to respond positively and innovatively to the new social aspirations, urges and problems of the people. It is often paralysed into inaction by pressures from the political executive on the one hand and the surging discontent of the people on the other. Despite the operation of forces and counter-forces like these no worth-while effort has been made either to deconcentrate political power or to restructure bureaucracy in a way that it takes on lesser responsibilities but performs with competence. The uneasy mix of political and bureaucratic power is responsible, in many ways, for ineffective performance or non-performance in development as well as in other key areas of normal government of a country.

This trend is evidently counter-productive. The common people have very limited or no access to the government. Even for the most essential contacts they invariably have to enlist the help of inter-mediaries – political brokers or middlemen. This is available for a price. To get things done people have to grease the palms of state functionaries at different levels; corruption appears to be built into the *modus operandi* of the emerging system. This generally breeds distrust of the machinery of the state. On the other hand, an insulated political and administrative system cannot perform well because it does not get adequate feedback from the grass-roots. Even when distress signals are loud and clear it tends to sidetrack them or to underestimate their importance. It is only when the fires of discontent turn into raging flames that it belatedly makes an effort to contain them. Lack of participation in the decision-making process generates apathy in the common people whose latent activism is exploited by anti-government forces in their own interest.

The Need for Institution Building

The situation could be rectified by imaginative institution building aimed at deconcentrating political power from the centre, reducing the role and responsibilities of the bureaucracy to manageable limits and enlisting the people's participation in decision making covering at least those areas that vitally concern local and regional problems. Some countries have made efforts to decentralize for development; but most of them have been half-hearted and hedged with too many reservations. Those entrenched in positions of political power look to the new institutional framework with distrust, for it might pose a threat to them. The bureaucracy, at least covertly, is hostile to new experiments. Having painfully learned to work with the new political masters – at the national and state levels a working equation between the two has been evolved – it is now suspicious about plans to add two or three new levels of decision making which are likely to complicate the situation further and require the bureaucracy to learn the techniques of working with the people and their institutions. So far it had governed the people and, in a gesture of generosity, even tried to work for the people; but working with them would pose new problems and would possibly result in further erosion of its already eroded power and authority. The experiment of *panchayati raj* – democratic decentralization – was not an unqualified success in India for it did not have either political support or bureaucratic determination to make it work. The fate of *basic democracy* in Pakistan was no different. True democratization at the local and regional level does not go well with an authoritarian regime at the centre.

In varying degrees this has been the experience of other countries where experiments of this nature have also been tried in one form or another. The élite at best gave only grudging support to the idea. The results are evident. Over-burdened governments and their executive arm continue to falter. Governments stand more for non-performance than for performance. To ensure access for the people to developmental and other relevant decision-making, to organize a built in system of adequate feedback and to ensure human resources mobilization through participation another effort at decentralization for development, through institution building, is necessary. This time there must be greater political will behind the move and all impediments to its success should be resolutely handled.

Another area of institution building relates to planning mechanisms and institutions. Over the years planning techniques in many Third World countries have improved, or at least acquired greater sophistication. The data base is more adequate and accurate. Three decades of experience have taught the planners that copying of models successfully used elsewhere does not work; a creative input that is culture- and problem-specific is needed. The shocks of repeated failures have generated much fresh thinking. Planning is no longer as conservative and orthodox as it used to be; it is now open to try, on a limited scale, some bold and even radical experiments. This is all for the good. However, some basic defects in planning institutions and procedures persist. The planners still work in remote ivory towers. They rely on masses of statistical data rather than on the feel of the pulse of the people. There is an unmistakable tendency to produce perfect and well rounded plans rather than plans that work. The elegance of the model and the refinement of methodology appeals to planners and as a consequence they produce impressive tomes that stand out for their seductive theoretic framework and impressive methodological rigour. As essential component of the plan suffers in this process: project formulation and project appraisal are invariably poor. The planner considers these menial chores beneath his dignity and leaves them to lesser state functionaries and implementing agencies. Plans often misfire because of this. The procedures of performance audit and evaluation leave much to be desired. Their results are not fed adequately, and in time, into planning processes. These drawbacks necessitate a thorough overhaul of planning mechanisms and institutions. This is the second important area of institution building and it should link up organically with the decentralized institutions set up for development.

Much planning and development in Third World countries is governed by the pragmatism of today's problems. There is either an absence of perspective or when an effort is made to evolve one it has a lack of depth. Such long-term views as exist are often ideologically loaded or tend to be negative. The obvious is stated with great flourish; but an adequate assembly of systematic data or hard thinking rarely forms part of these exercises. For several key areas of development status reports or state-of-the-art analyses are either not available or are deficient. The spectrum of policy options is not clearly worked out in terms of costs and benefits, estimates of diverse reactions and obstacles and projections of long-range consequences. Vital areas of development are studied in isolation from one another and their linkages are not systematically spelled out. Different academic specialities tend to pull in different directions and in consequence a holistic and organic picture of the situation does not emerge. The planning apparatus does make some efforts in this direction; but most of them are feeble because of the absence of high talent resources to do so. The links between the planning sector and the academic sector are tenuous and are confined generally to occasional meetings for exchange of ideas. Meaningful and sustained research that could feed into the policy processes is either not carried out or its results come out too late to be an input of value to plan formulation.

It is not suggested that all research should be geared to planning; scholars must have freedom to pursue lines of enquiries that appear important to them or interest them. None the less the requirements of planning and development cannot be totally ignored, especially when research enjoys massive financial support from the state. There is evidence that Third World scholarship is becoming increasingly aware of this responsibility. A great communication gap persists, however, between the planners and the academics. The former cannot articulate their research needs properly and the academics cannot present their findings in a format that could be used readily by the planner. Operationalizing research results remains a baffling problem. The academic, by nature, functions as a social critic. This is not to be deprecated; but too much negativity and pessimism is of little use to the development planner. Social criticism should transcend the narrow grooves within which much of it operates: it is not enough to say *what* is wrong, it is also necessary to bring out *why* it is wrong and *how* the situation can be rectified. Institutionalizing the linkage between planning on the one hand and research and reflection on the other in such a manner that basic objectives are shared and the interchange of ideas and insights becomes mutually meaningful and relevant is a priority.

In many diverse areas of life that are functionally specific there is a good case for minimal state interference and for according autonomy and responsibility to the institutions best suited to deal with them. This would be a step in the direction of deconcentration of power and allocation of responsibilities and decision-making to sectors where they belong. State support would be needed, but in the process the state must operate under some self-denying regulations so as not to erode the functional autonomy of these institutions. There is cheerless evidence of a near institutional collapse because of too many stifling government regulations and frequent interference. Excellence has to be pursued and problem-solving exercises have to be undertaken; this can best be done in an atmosphere of freedom. The institutions that already exist have to be revamped and new institutions set up and carefully nursed. This would bring out the best from the creative segments of the society which unfortunately at present have a feeling of being neglected and in consequence are becoming increasingly alienated.

To sum up, what is being suggested is rethinking the entire institutional framework of society, especially in relation to power, with a view to renovating and rebuilding some structures and innovating others. Deconcentration of power and authority is a must, at least in the larger countries; decentralization for development will contribute, we hope, to the removal of the hiatus between the planners and the people and will provide a more propitious setting for relevant and smooth development.

What is needed, first, is the creation of multilevel institutions geared mainly to developmental decision making, but sharing also some authority and responsibilities in other areas of administration. This network of institutions will be aimed mainly at allowing increased access for the people to both development agencies and general administration, ensuring their participation in decisions that concern their present life as well as their future and contributing to their civic and political education through the experience of setting development priorities and targets as well as of lending a helping hand in the implementation of the plans and in the realization of their objectives. The new institutional structure that is envisaged will provide a significant boost to human resources mobilization; ensure an adequate feedback; and help focus attention on the specificities of the local and regional aspirations; priorities and development needs. To make such an experiment successful, it would be necessary to support it with faith and trust in the people. Too many reservations or too much caution will never let these institutions take-off. There must be real delegation of powers and margin should be allowed for people to make mistakes. Experience is a great teacher. The people will not be able to develop their associational capability if their initiatives are curbed by frequent political and administrative interference or if bureaucracy, doubtless with good intentions, is encouraged to wet-nurse them. Imaginative orientation and training programmes, however, will be necessary. They will have threefold functions: raising and enlarging the consciousness of the people, imparting competence and skills to them in functional areas and encouraging them to depoliticize local and regional issues and problems on whose desirability and necessity there could be consensus.

The second area that calls for urgent attention is the restructuring of public services. A fresh look is required on the recruitment process and procedures, training and continuous retraining, and development of co-ordinated work norms. The eternal conflict between the generalist administrators and the technical specialists will have to be resolved satisfactorily. Special attention will have to be given to the creation of a new operating culture in which there is devolution of authority and responsibilities, simplification and rationalization of procedures, encouragement to innovation and a reward for effective problem solving. There should be opportunities and encouragement for public servants to specialize and the structure should be sufficiently open and flexible to be able to draw special competence and expertise at the higher levels even from outside the ranks of the bureaucratic hierarchy.

As suggested earlier, the third area in need of reform is planning mechanisms and institutions. To ensure success of the planning enterprise several steps will have to be contemplated. The data base will have to be strengthened and feedback mechanisms streamlined. The quality of project formulation and appraisal will have to be vastly upgraded and implementational capability fortified. The planners cannot give up their concern for the immediate present, but at the same time they cannot absolve themselves from the responsibilities of long-term planning. This requires building bridges of understanding and communication between the planning sector and the academic sector. Planning must also provide for performance audit and evaluation and should be informed and guided by them. Additionally, it must inform and educate people with regard to its goals and instrumentalities as well as setbacks and successes.

Finally, in diverse functional areas a network of institutions should be allowed to function and flourish with autonomy and self-respect. Where they do not exist they should be set up. For their success the politician and the bureaucrat must restrain themselves from a display of arrogance of power and celebration of ignorance. Frequent shifts in goals will have to be held in check and a culture of excellence assiduously promoted.

Difficulties and Problems

Institution building is an infinitely complex and difficult task and requires a great deal of imagination, patience and perseverance. Many difficulties can be anticipated. Established thought patterns and working methods will tend to persist. Vested interests will assert themselves as they will not want to surrender the power and prestige they currently enjoy. The tendency to distrust institutional innovation is common. There may be political reservations about the new institutional framework and also fear of negative social consequences. It is possible that the multilevel institutions suggested will get heavily politicized and will not perform their explicit objectives; instead they will devote themselves to another set of covert goals which run counter to the purpose for which they were originally set up. It is also likely that entrenched vested interests may try to capture these institutions and re-assert themselves through the new power and prestige derived through them. There is a possibility that the creation of such institutions may be a ritual act endowed only with a symbolic significance and not involving a genuine transfer of power and responsibilities. Similarly, bureaucracy may be uncooperative and even obstructive in order to hold on to what remains of its already eroded power and privilege. At a time when government is becoming an unending chain of fire-fighting operations and has been reduced to the position of having to handle one crisis after another, alibis and rationalization can be found for not tampering with the planning apparatus. In the area of planning, too, the calculus of power is likely to prevail. The absence of consensus on national objectives will keep planning a subject of political debate and controversy, open to attack on political grounds irrespective of the merit and quality of the plans it formulates. Governments may seek to control and manipulate other institutions for reasons of patronage. Thus, institution building may only receive lip service.

Comment

Admittedly, institutional change is not easy; but it has to be understood that in the ultimate reckoning the cost of no change is much greater than the cost of the change that is suggested. If the present situation is allowed to continue it will result in chaos at the top and anaemia at the extremities. The centre will have much more than it can attend to efficiently and effectively; the periphery will remain voiceless even about decisions that vitally concern its present and future. The more the centre adds to its power and responsibilities, the less it will be in a position to accomplish. In consequence more problems will remain unsolved, contributing to greater frustration and unrest among the people. The deglamourized and much harassed bureaucracy already stands discredited; it will be still further discredited if it single-handedly tries to cope with tasks whose magnitude is increasing manifold and for particular sectors of which it has no competence. Because of the denial of access and participation to the people in planning and implementation of developmental change, the present precipitous position will continue to prevail. The planners will continue to have an élite bias and lopsided priorities. They will foist unwanted reforms and their handling of local and regional issues will invariably be poor. In India, Pakistan and Bangladesh they have been unable to mobilize human and physical resources adequately; in order to maintain a semblance of performance they continue the policy of development by subsidies. This results in a loss of the people's initiative, and also in the erosion of their self-esteem. Without a long-range, in depth and multidimensional perspective planning will lose much of its force and relevance. A society that does not give adequate attention to sharpening its problem-solving capabilities and promoting excellence is destined to lag behind in the race for progress. Much will be lost if the opportunity for real development through institution building is given up only for fear of some of its temporarily unsettling consequences.

Notes

1. *World Development Report*, World Bank, Washington, DC, 1980.
2. *World Development Report*, World Bank, Washington, DC, 1978.
3. Friere, Paolo, *The Pedagogy of the Oppressed*, Harmondsworth, Penguin, 1972.
4. Lewis, Oscar, "The Culture of Poverty", *Scientific American*, vol. 215, no. 4, October 1966.
5. Leeds, Anthony, "The Concept of the 'Culture of Poverty': Conceptual, Logical, and Empirical Problems with Perspective from Brazil and Peru, in Eleanor Burke Leacock, (ed.) *The Culture of Poverty: a Critique*, New York, Simon and Schuster, 1970.
6. Illich, Ivan, *The Deschooling Society*, New York, Harper and Row, 1971.

7   Summing Up

In the decades following the end of the Second World War, the Third World has experienced several changes of mood, but in respect of economic growth and technological change – or, development generally – it has moved from euphoria to despair. During this period its dream world has been shattered; its newly gained political independence had failed to usher the promised era of plenty and prosperity. This has caused anguish to the people whose revolution of rising expectations has turned into a nightmare of mounting frustrations. The modernizing élite has found itself in a chastened mood; its planning and development strategies have faltered and failed. With a trail of unrealized utopias behind, development has lost its mystique. The collapse of the classical paradigm of development has urged serious rethinking as well as a search for alternatives.

Soon after the break-up of empires and the emergence of sovereign and independent nations in their place, ambitious schemes for national development were launched. Development was the magic of transformation – the twentieth-century Aladdin's lamp. People's hopes were fed by the corps of development experts who arrived on the scene. The diagnostic efforts were mostly superficial. The remedies they offered were largely untried, but they were promoted with a confidence that would put to shame the pushers of oriental potency potions. In retrospect, it is inescapably obvious that their faith in development was simplistic and their understanding of the developmental process bordered on naivete. With every passing year the "experts" realized that the notion of the inevitability of progress was a myth, that the calculus of economics alone led to misdirection of effort, that the human factor enmeshed in the social and cultural ethos was a force to contend with and that subtle political considerations intervening in the development process, if not sensitively managed, could bring disaster. In the brief span of only two decades, development thinking changed both in spirit and substance; from unreserved and limitless faith in development being able to find solutions to all their problems, the "experts" now heard, with awe and respect, the counsel of despair that questioned the very desirability of development and projected it as enemy number one of society. The counter-developmental ideology made a powerful impact on a section of Third World intellectuals.

A slightly less pessimistic mood was represented by those who, though not ready to banish development, were willing to consider the impossibility of it beyond a point. The persuasive logic of limits to growth was a sobering influence on them. Yet another school of thought pleaded with considerable force that a change in the direction and pace of development was imperative. Even the most optimistic among those concerned with national strategies of development realized that the much heralded paradigm of development, with which they started, was sterile and that both developmental objectives and strategies required rethinking. This recognition led also to reflection on humanity's possible futures, on a preferred future, and on alternatives. Concepts like "another development" or "second development" began to emerge.

Though some of these exercises had a certain utopian quality about them, they were informed by an assessment of our contemporary predicament and sought to map out guidelines for action which could counter identifiable obstacles and restructure society for the realization of new goals. In the process, there was an unquestionable paradigm shift. But the emerging paradigms were themselves wobbly and were groping towards a variety of interlinked objectives that were fraught with many intangibles. Some of this thinking did reflect a serious concern and search – concern for a future with an order characterized by autonomy and equity, and search for viable strategies for the realization of the new goals. These reflective endeavours were not without snags: the new vision did not demonstrate how it would deal with entrenched interests and prevailing power equations that created opposition between the developed and the underdeveloped and caused development in two-thirds of the world to take place within a framework of dependency. The suspicion that some of these utopias were the products of clever manipulation and were deftly projected to perpetuate the duality with a view to distracting the Third World from its quest for a just share of world resources and a position of equality in global decision-making processes is not entirely without foundation.

The principal reasons for the failure of the paradigm of developmentalism are easy to identify. Both in the global and the national contexts the developmental process was bound to be unequal. In the international setting, it was weighted in favour of the rich and powerful nations who sought to maintain a barely disguised colonial relationship with the underdeveloped countries. The contemporary North–South formulation raises the issues of inequality of resources and power; some of its premises may be open to debate and its conclusions unconvincing, but it does bring into clear relief a number of key issues that can no longer be brushed aside. In the Third World countries themselves small centres have grown at the expense of a large periphery, which has remained impoverished and anaemic. The dominant centres of power – economic and political – favour pockets of prosperity and deal with underdeveloped areas as if they were their internal colonies. Paradoxically, development has made the weaker sections of society more vulnerable.

It has been convincingly demonstrated that a small number of developed countries have cornered for themselves a disproportionately large share of the world's developmental resources. In consequence, the wherewithal of development available to the less developed world is woefully small and even its most efficient utilization is not likely to register impressive gains.

Developmental aid is not as humanitarian as it is often made out to be; the invisible strings attached to it are exploitative and are aimed at the maintenance of the neocolonial pattern of relationships. Trade, on unequal and unfavourable terms, can hardly be expected to contribute to development in any significant measure. Both aid and trade reinforce the dependency relationship.

This inequality of development is also visible in the less developed countries: around small islands of dazzling affluence there is a cheerless ocean of poverty and degradation. Even in the developed countries, in distributive terms, the spread of benefits of development can be demonstrated to be inequitable; in the less developed countries the contrasts are glaring and dramatic. Egalitarianism and social justice, in practice, are ideals without content, promises not seriously intended. They are goals that tantalizingly recede into the background as limited developmental objectives are achieved. There are sharp contrasts in the want–have ratio for the rich and the poor; the two poles represent two separate worlds. The number of those below the subsistence level increases rather than diminishes. Alongside this absolute poverty, there is mounting evidence of increasing unemployment. Official documents detailing the spread of social services offer, at best, only statistical satisfaction; these achievements are merely notional.

The culture of poverty is accentuated by the poverty of plans for cultural enrichment, including development of a critical consciousness. Thus, programmes geared to meet the minimum needs of the people skirt round the gut issues they are intended to tackle. In practice, they impart the superficial veneer of a mass-oriented approach that is more populist than radical. Unfulfilled aspirations lead to frustrations that cause tensions and turmoil. The apparatus for managing tension and conflict is feeble, distinguished more for its non-performance than for its achievement. Even when the less developed countries wish to correct the imbalances in their strategies, they find themselves helpless; they discover, to their dismay, that many developmental decisions are taken outside their boundaries. Colonialism may be dead but neocolonialism persists and is becoming more powerful. Invisible strings are so skilfully pulled that the principal actors on the national development scene can only perform like marionettes. The linkages between power centres in the developed world and the modernizing élite in the developing world are firmly established; the vested interests in the latter, in crises, get powerful support from their foreign patrons.

Development is an infinitely complex process. Developmental goals are not easily translated into reality. Attractively packaged formulations get hamstrung at critical turns. The charisma of leaders produces mobilization, but it rarely produces development. If rhetoric and hyperbole were enough to result in development, by now the Third World would have regained paradise. But we are painfully aware that the reality is different. If developmental endeavours in many of the less developed countries have proved sterile, serious reflection on the factors underlying pseudo-policy and pseudo-performance, which are in many ways worse than non-policy and non-performance, is called for.

The critical areas that need to be probed in this context are the mechanics of decision making, the creation of conditions of development and the evolution of an infrastructure and institutional framework for sustained growth and its redistribution.

Consider first the dynamics of decision making. The vital question in this context is who decides for whom. A great deal of developmental decision making has been characterized by an élite bias, which results in unwanted reforms, neglect of the vital needs of the neediest, and brave populist plan projections for which the management capability does not exist. A substantial part of the planning endeavour concentrates on output goals and projects; social goals get articulated *sotto voce*. There is a noticeable concentration on increasing the value of the GNP. Experience suggests that this emphasis on the aggregate of marketable goods and services undervalues the full production of a society, resulting in the narrowing of the social roles and significance of large sections of the population. Worse still, such an approach underplays the vital question of distribution. Economic growth is assumed to take care of cultural and social needs. This assumption, however, has proved fallacious. The trickle down effect, in practice, is found to be minimal; the invisible hand does not work. It is necessary to evolve an adequate cultural/social policy, which takes account of the social needs of the weak and the vulnerable sections and harmonize it with the economic policy. Unless economic policy is geared to well considered social objectives, its results are likely to be counter-productive. Participative decision making in formulating social objectives and outlining the means for their attainment can correct many of the imbalances and distortions that characterize the planners' plans, which in many ways are far removed from the social reality of the day.

Afflicted with endemic poverty, the masses lack the critical awareness to join in the debate and assert themselves. The planners take their cue from politicians who often deliberately distort the perception of the poor about their own social reality. To politicians, political survival is paramount. This forces them to ignore the long-term perspective and resort to gimmicks that offer instant satisfaction and concentrate on short-range policies to serve survival needs. Notable exceptions apart, not many in the ranks of leadership have an understanding of the intricacies and inner dimensions of major policy issues and their long-term intended and unintended ramifications and consequences. The generalist administrator often over-rates his undeniable but limited competence. His capabilities in the area of policy making need to be sharpened and enriched considerably. The experts perhaps know their field in some depth; but not many of them are sensitized to the needs of policy making and to its political and administrative overtones. These three segments can often be seen to work at cross-purposes; fusion of their resources and insights, so necessary for successful policy making and its implementation, is rarely achieved. None of the three is sufficiently responsive to the sensitivities of the people for whom, in the last analysis, the development endeavour is really intended and who remain voiceless.

Consider also the external influences that contribute to the shaping of national policies in less developed countries. Sometimes they are unobtrusive and invisible; often they are aggressively visible and domineeringly evident. It is now established that foreign aid is not a reflection of human compassion or of the goodwill of the privileged for the underprivileged; it usually reflects the national interests of the donor country and in critical situations can show itself as blatant imperialism. Ordinary citizens in the developed countries evince a genuine concern, but their contribution does not materially alter the underlying effects of foreign aid. Large-scale deployment of international expertise has been, in many ways, dysfunctional and even damaging. It has resulted in fixing of lopsided priorities, faulty technology choice, adoption of inapplicable and irrelevant strategies, subversion of minds and accentuation of dependency relationships. It is true that in the world of today some patterns of interdependence are inevitable; but they must evolve on the basis of equality and not generate humiliating patterns of patron–client relationships. Many distortions in fixing of short-term and long-range targets, critical decisions regarding resource allocation and inputs, redefinition of objectives and recognition of priorities and adoption of management strategies have been a consequence of the advice of the high gods of international aid, many of whom have been exposed as ignoramuses. If nothing else, they certainly inhibited endogenous growth and sought to perpetuate unequal relationships. The many blueprints of a new international order have implicit in them correctives to those imbalances and disharmonies that have clearly emerged in the last decade.

Hiring of international expertise for policy making is a short cut to cover the inadequacies of the national planning apparatus or else a function of a binational or multinational understanding. Its pay-off has not been impressive for some very obvious reasons. It has been suggested earlier that these high priced experts – advisers and consultants – cannot wholly divorce themselves from their national interests. Their services are often part of a package deal and they have to safeguard the terms and spirit of the aid or loan which brings them to the less developed countries. This is not all. Many of them find themselves working in a totally alien and unfamiliar cultural milieu and are puzzled by the political and cultural environment in which they have to operate. Socialization in the home environment has established their thought patterns and they tend to apply their past experience to the new situation they are handling. Many of their endeavours remain fruitless because their ideas cannot take root in the new cultural soil. They blame social institutions, cultural norms and values for their failure. Not many of them realize that these are more difficult to change than technology or economic practices. Cultural self-image and identity resist changes in their hard core.

Native planners, rather than making a creative response to the challenges of their social reality, tend to work on borrowed models picked up from high prestige centres of learning abroad or from reigning concepts and theories. This provides an excellent example of captive minds at work. In their task they encounter a variety of other difficulties. For some critical areas of planning benchmarks do not exist; statistics are inadequate and often unreliable. Most administrators, trained for general administration, are unfamiliar with techniques of macro- and micro-planning. Their blueprints for different sectors and sub-sectors do not enmesh. Thus, we often have a series of discrete plans that are individually passable but which, because of the absence of fit between them, cannot stand together as an integrated national plan. This also explains why employment-, poverty- and need-oriented programmes lack vision and dynamism. Think tanks of men and women of knowledge and foresight, who could weigh and evaluate possible policy options and chart action guidelines involving minimum costs, do not exist. Nor are any efforts made to create such pools capability. Several elements of the current and the emerging political idiom, which are obstacles to long-range planning, cannot be wished away. They often impart an *ad hoc* character to policy endeavours and in some contexts reduce them to exercises intended only to meet one crisis after the other. Coordination is weak, monitoring ineffective and evaluation shallow. Evaluation techniques currently in use lack depth and perspective; most of them barely scratch the surface. So much of the time of planners and administrators is spent in tension management and its spin-offs that they cannot apply their minds to cool consideration of the crises that are likely to occur in the future. These crises, it may be added, are likely to be of greater intensity and increased frequency in the years to come. As such, the importance of efforts at developing a unified policy science cannot be over-emphasized.

The other two critical areas – creation of conditions of development and evolution of infrastructure and institutional framework for sustained growth and its distributive dimension – are closely interrelated and can best be considered together.

In contemporary social science literature focused on development several hypotheses covering the attitudinal–motivational and organizational–institutional frameworks of development have been offered. With the wisdom of hindsight, generated by three decades of experience, they look unconvincing. In any case, most of them need to be reconsidered. While some important economic prerequisites of growth have been identified the thinking about the social and cultural prerequisites is still unclear. Rationality leads to modernization but modernization, in its turn, also contributes to a greater degree of rationality. The notion of rationality itself needs rethinking; its meaning changes in different contexts and there are several levels of rationality. It is realized that empathy, mobility and high participation contribute to development in a significant way; but it should also be recognized that conditions of underdevelopment inhibit the growth of these attributes. No workable guidelines exist for developing them. Communication and education may promote them, under certain conditions; but they are both known also to harden existing prejudices and predispositions. Relative deprivation may inspire efforts at development, but it also promotes passivity and fatalism. The case of *n*-Achievement motivation – the desire to excel irrespective of the felt desire for rewards – has been over-argued; all its consequences may not be socially desirable. Being essentially self-oriented, it is likely to preclude a community orientation. Besides some of the ways suggested to promote it border on the ridiculous. Can it really be promoted by crash programmes of short duration? Rational ends–means calculations and calculated risk taking are essential for growth, but in a culture of poverty people are known to hold fast to the precarious security offered by tradition.

Institutions such as the extended family, castes and religion have been blamed for the backwardness of the economy and for the general lack of dynamism in society. The criticism is perhaps partially valid; but the critics do not say how we can eradicate or even erode them with a view to preparing the ground for speedy development. It is more likely that such institutions – and the attitude patterns associated with them – will undergo major transformations and adapt to the emerging milieu when a significant degree of economic development has taken place. So far development experts have played largely by hunches, many of which remain untested hypotheses. It is to be noted that these diagnoses remain silent about the inequitable world economic order and the oppressive structural characteristics of the developing societies. This conspiracy of silence has blocked a meaningful discussion of the real issues of development in the Third World.

The entire spectrum of deficiencies enumerated above is attributed to the "culture of poverty", which accounts for low achievement motivation, failure to conceptualize progress and unwillingness to take risks. In such a cultural setting people lack innovativeness, become fatalistic and do not see the point of deferring present gratification for future advantage. They have a limited world view; their interpersonal relations are characterized by a low degree of empathy and great mutual distrust. The poor often explain their condition as one inflicted on them by fate or relate it to their innate deficiencies; the traditional world view and value system support this perception. This erroneous view of the culture of poverty holds that the condition of the poor is an outcome of their self-inflicted deficiencies and that it can be changed by transmission of new information and skills. The oppressive and exploitative nature of the economic and socio-political system is never highlighted as the primary cause of poverty and degradation.

The characteristics of the culture of poverty, at the same time, are rarely explained as the response of the poor to the prevailing social condition and not the cause of their poverty. What is not understood is that poverty is self-perpetuating not because its environment and values have been created by the poor, but because of the wider structural framework determined by the economic and political impositions of the non-poor. It is because of the imperatives of the social situation – primarily absence of work and very low incomes – that the poor have to adapt to the extremely limited resources at their disposal. This leads to compliance and silence regarding the sub-human conditions of their lives. New information and skills can do little to alter the situation. This has been proved in almost all areas of development activity. No satisfactory progress in agriculture or cottage industries has been achieved. Despite new knowledge, family planning programmes and health programmes have not made much headway. Where earning two square meals a day is an achievement, it is ridiculous to expect the poor to defer gratification, or to have a margin of savings, or to take risks in investments.

Developmental approaches, covertly supporting the status quo, have not been able to make any appreciable dent in the volume of poverty. Even in India, which proudly claims to be the tenth most industrialized nation of the world, the number of those living in absolute poverty has remained stationary (according to some it has actually increased). In much of the Third World the situation is broadly the same. This deplorable condition prevails despite three decades of development in which extension agencies have been doing their best to pass on information and inculcate skills. The poor remain poor because they have unequal access to land, irrigation, health services and education, because rural wages are low and year-round employment is difficult to find, and because the new structure of economic opportunities is practically closed to them. Having to adapt to an economy of precarious security, they attribute their condition either to supernatural forces or to their own inherent limitations. Their perceptions are reinforced by the oppressive minority which stands to gain from the maintenance of the status quo and would lose many of its advantages if a critical consciousness developed among the poor, who would then begin to see the exploitative character of the social structure. The array of concepts and theories offered by the social sciences have failed to recognize this very obvious factor which is the crux of the problem. The lines of exploration pursued by them are not entirely worthless; but their utility is limited by the fact they are not directly aimed at obviating efforts at radical structural alterations focused on eradication of the exploitation and oppression that perpetuate poverty.

Even at the risk of repetition, let us recapitulate the main propositions of this study. The growth strategies of the first three decades having gone awry, rethinking goals and strategies of development, both in the developed and the underdeveloped countries, has emerged as a major human concern. The paradigm with which these endeavours were initiated and pursued for over thirty years stands self-condemned. Although it has not been replaced the principal ingredients of an alternative can now be identified.

First, many of the conceptual cobwebs surrounding development have to be cleared and the notion redefined. Economic growth undeniably tops the agenda for development, but a consideration of its distributional dimension is also a must. While urging and supporting plans for economic growth, it is necessary to keep in mind their broad human and social objectives. In other words, the vital question to be constantly asked is, economic growth for what? The goals will have to be set in terms of enrichment of the quality of life, giving high priority to meeting the basic needs of those living in absolute poverty and constituting nearly one-half of the Third World. Investment in people is as necessary as input for economic growth. Meanwhile, a careful watch will have to be maintained on rapidly depleting non-renewable resources and environmental constraints will have to be borne in mind. Western levels of affluence and consumption may not be possible or even desirable; alternative patterns ensuring a satisfactory and full life can be evolved. The targets can be reset from time to time and raised to progressively higher levels; the beginning, of course, will have to be modest. There is no point in setting our sights impossibly high; development must be sustainable.

Second, within the national context of development, attention will have to be given to the central problem of the eradication first of absolute poverty and then of poverty generally. It has been convincingly demonstrated that poverty lies at the root of most of the problems the Third World faces: The explanations of poverty that have dominated the social science scene so far have been inadequate; the strategy of making inputs in information and skills has not paid off. The situation is likely to deteriorate if the present structures, which perpetuate and reinforce exploitation and oppression, are not demolished. A dynamic approach to structural change, therefore, must receive high priority in all plans of development. This is a prerequisite to successful solution of the problem of poverty; welfarism is no answer. The strategies should reflect a creative and endogenous response to the challenges of the contemporary social reality by dissociating themselves from the set patterns of thought that have hampered progress so far. Planning and implementation mechanisms will have to be radically modified.

Third, even the most well intentioned efforts at institution building geared to allowing access to the poor to the processes of planning and to the fruits of development are likely to founder if they are not backed by imaginative programmes of conscientization. The common people must know their rights and understand their responsibilities. Politicization without conscientization, as many developing countries are beginning to learn at great cost, is counter-productive. Conscientization and education hold the key to effective human resource mobilization and participative decision making. They also lead to relevant institution building; rejecting in the process grandiose élite-imposed structures that do not work. An additional advantage would be that people themselves would be able to determine the right mix of endogenous and exogenous elements in the goals and paths of change.

Fourth, to ensure equal participation in development a policy of affirmative action – positive discrimination – is indicated. Without it conditions of genuine equality of opportunity cannot be brought about. The policy should cover all deprived sections of society, including women. This should be visualized essentially as a preparatory mechanism and not allowed to degenerate into support for a parasitical class.

Fifth, a closer and critical look at the institutional structure is indicated. Western-type democratic institutions have collapsed in several Third World countries; in some others they are only a facade. Even where they have proved durable, they are problem ridden. A viable alternative has to be found. The largely colonial administrative structures of most developing countries will have to be reorganized so that they become more sensitive and responsive to development needs. The gap between plan formulation on the one hand and project preparation and appraisal on the other is a wide one: plans are often sophisticated and systematic, project formulation is clumsy and appraisal ineffective. Administrative restructuring, and especially its training component, will need considerable renovation and innovation. It will be necessary to find out why earlier efforts in this field proved sterile so that suitable correctives can be applied.

Sixth, a package of measures will have to be contemplated for the management of the socio-cultural environment, which because of its growing viciousness is making both government and development difficult. Many of these problems can be attributed to lack or inadequacy of development; but some of them are the by-products of the process of development itself or its innate deficiencies. The story does not end here. Immature politics, focused on the pragmatism of dealing with today's problems, feeds the fires of discontent and obfuscates perspective planning for the next 25 years and beyond. It also leads to preoccupation with fire-fighting chores and the picking of soft options. Add to this the forces of destabilization and subversion introduced from without and the magnitude of the task becomes immense; but unless we come to grips with it counter-development is likely to result.

Finally, the global context of development will have to be re-examined. So long as the prevailing unequal access to resources continues, nothing can be done to dismantle the great divide between the rich and the poor countries. There really are only two worlds – a small world of the rich and a much larger world of the poor – although within this bipolar world some other poles can also be identified. All projections appear to suggest that if the prevailing trends persist the gulf dividing these two worlds will have been considerably widened, not narrowed, as we enter the 21st Century. The prospects for sub-Saharan Africa and South Asia are specially bleak. It is fashionable to talk of one planet and one environment: it is about time we begin to think of one humanity. Together with more equitable sharing of resources, all other manifestations of superordinate and subordinate relationships between the developed and the developing countries will also have to be attended to. There can be no true partnership in development on the basis of unequal relationships.

It is undeniable that a substantial part of the total available human resources, rather than being applied to improve the human condition, is being directed to heavy armaments enhancing our potential for self-destruction. If diverted to constructive uses, our ingenuity could find solutions to the baffling problems of misery and degradation of nearly two-thirds of humanity. Affluence breeds a great deal of other wasteful expenditure. A part of it at least can be put to productive use to help find solutions to nagging problems that have plagued humanity for centuries. One to two per cent of the GNP of the industrialized countries, if it were diverted to problem-solving uses, could work miracles for the Third World. It would not only alleviate human suffering but would hold in check the forces of destabilization that are likely to emerge, in the foreseeable future, as a threat to us all. And this would be no charity to the Third World, nor even compensation for the resources extorted from it during the colonial phase to make the development of the West possible. If the industrialized countries want to use the non-renewable resources from the Third World, they must be willing to pay a realistic price. This would result not only in substantial transfer of resources to the developing countries but would also be a step towards restraining the rapid depletion of scarce resources. A fair share, on population basis, must accrue to the Third World from the profits of the exploitation of our common resources. Conservation of resources must begin at the level of the affluent countries who have been consuming them at an alarming rate. Similarly, the problem of conservation of ecological and environmental balance is more acute in the world of the super-affluent. It is they who must come out with plans of effective control. But it would be futile to expect voluntary renunciation, even of a limited degree, from the highly industrialized countries. Logic and reason may be on the side of the Third World, but it is weak and disunited. Unless it develops collective muscle, it will not be able to bargain from a position of strength. Polemics and rhetoric score only debating points.

At the same time, patterns of intra-Third World cooperation – to begin with on a sub-regional and regional basis – must be evolved and strengthened. This cooperation must not be restricted only to trade and industry; new frontiers of Third World self-reliance should be explored ceaselessly. By pooling of resources – human and financial – the Third World can take steps to close the widening scientific and technological gap between the developed and the underdeveloped. Third World brain power and trained skills are making no mean contribution to progress in the West: given a propitious climate of work and the right incentives they can be brought back to Third World institutions to undertake relevant research, both fundamental and applied.

Development today poses a challenge and presents an opportunity. Urgent reflection and action are needed for our very survival is at stake. Modernization is not possible on the basis of its original paradigm which implicitly legitimizes inequality and injustice.

Bibliography*

Modernization

Almond, Gabriel and G. Bingham Powel, *Comparative Politics: Systems, Process and Policy* (2nd ed.), Boston, MA, Little, Brown, 1978.

Arnon, I. and M. Raviv, *From Fellah to Farmer: A Study on Change in Arab Villages*, Rehovot, Settlement Study Center, 1980.

Aron, Raymond, *The Industrial Society: Three Essays on Ideology and Development*, New York, Praeger, 1967.

Arora, Satish K., "Pre-empted Future? Notes on Theories of Political Development," *Behavioural Sciences and Community Development*, 2 September 1968, pp. 85–120.

Banks, David J. (ed.), *Changing Identities in Modern Southeast Asia*, The Hague, Mouton, 1976.

Bell, Daniel, *The Coming of Post-industrial Society: A Venture in Social Forecasting*, New York, Basic Books, 1973.

Bellah, Robert N. (ed.), *Religion and Progress in Modern Asia*, New York, Free Press, 1965.

Black, Cyril E. (ed.), *Comparative Modernization: A Reader*, New York, Free Press, 1976.

Braibanti, Ralph and Joseph J. Spengler (eds), *Tradition, Values and Socioeconomic Development*, Durham, NC, Duke University Press, 1961.

Coleman, J.R., *Comparative Economic Systems*, New York, Holt, Rinehart and Winston, 1968.

Dean, G.C., *Science and Technology for Development: Technology Policy and Industrialization in the People's Republic of China*, Ottawa, International Development Research Centre, 1979.

Dube, S.C., *India's Changing Villages: Human Factors in Community Development*, London, Routledge and Kegan Paul, 1958.

* This bibliography was prepared by Agnes How, Librarian of the United Nations Asian and Pacific Development Centre, Kuala Lumpur, with the assistance of Siti Rafeah Shamsuddin. It covers comprehensively most of the themes dealt with in this book.

Eisenstadt, S.N., *Modernization: Protest and Change*, Englewood Cliffs, NJ, Prentice Hall, 1966.

Ensminger, Douglas, *Rural India in Transition*, New Delhi, All India Panchayat Parishad, 1972.

Etzioni, Amitai and Eva Etzioni (eds), *Social Change: Sources, Patterns and Consequences*, New York, Basic Books, 1964.

Evers, Hans-Dieter (ed.), *Modernization in South-East Asia*, Kuala Lumpur, Oxford University Press, 1973.

————, *Sociology of South-East Asia: Readings on Social Change and Development*, Kuala Lumpur, Oxford University Press, 1980.

Foster, George M., *Traditional Societies and Technological Change* (2nd ed.), New York, Harper and Row, 1973.

Geertz, Clifford, *Peddlers and Princes: Social Change and Modernization in two Indonesian Towns*, Chicago, Chicago University Press, 1963.

Germani, Gino, *Social Modernization and Economic Development in Argentina*, Geneva, United Nations Research Institute for Social Development, 1970.

Hagen, Everett E., *The Economics of Development* (3rd ed.), Homewood, IL, Irwin, 1980.

Hellwege, J., "Under-development, Dependencia and Modernization Theory," *Law and State*, vol. 17, 1978, pp. 45–69.

Hernes, Gudmund, "Structural Change in Social Processes," *American Journal of Sociology*, vol. 82, no. 3, November 1976, pp. 513–47.

Hoselitz, Bert F. and Wilbert R. More (eds), *Industrialization and Society*, Paris, Mouton, 1963.

Hunter, Guy, *Modernizing Peasant Societies: A Comparative Study in Asia and Africa*, New York, Oxford University Press, 1969.

Huntington, Samuel P., "The Change to Change: Modernization, Development and Politics," *Comparative Politics*, vol. 3, April 1971, pp. 283–322.

Hussein Alatas, Syed, *Modernization and Social Change: Studies in Modernization, Religion, Social Change and Development in South-East Asia*, London, Angus and Robertson, 1972.

Inkeles, Alex and David H. Smith, *Becoming Modern: Individual Change in Six Developing Countries*, Cambridge, MA, Harvard University Press, 1974.

Irwin, Patrick H., "An Operational Definition of Societal Modernization," *Economic Development and Cultural Change*, vol. 23, no. 4, July 1975, pp. 595–613.

Jacobs, Norman, *Modernization Without Development: Thailand as an Asian Case Study*, New York, Praeger, 1971.

Kothari, Rajni, *State and Nation Building: A Third World Perspective*, Columbia, MO, South Asia Books, 1976.

————, State Building in the Third World: Alternative Strategies," *Economic and Political Weekly*, vol. 7, nos 5/7, February 1972.

Landsberger, Henry A. (ed.), *Rural Protest: Peasant Movements and Social Change*, London, Macmillan, 1974.

Lerner, Daniel, *The Passing of Traditional Society: Modernizing the Middle East*, Glencoe, IL, The Free Press, 1962.

Levy, Marion J., *Modernization and the Structure of Society: A Setting for International Affairs*, Princeton, NJ, Princeton University Press, 1966.

Lim Teck Ghee and Vincent Lowe (eds), *Towards a Modern Asia: Aims, Resources and Strategies*, Kuala Lumpur, Heinemann, 1967.

Mann, R.S., *Social Structure, Social Change and Future Trends: Indian Village Perspective*, Jaipur, Rawat Publications, 1979.

Mason, Edward S. et al. *The Economic and Social Modernization of the Republic of Korea*, Cambridge, MA, Council on East Asian Studies, Harvard University, 1980.

McClelland, David C., *Achieving Society*, New York, Halsted Press, 1976.

Mesthene, Emmanual G., *Technological Change: Its Impact on Man and Society*, Cambridge, MA, Harvard University Press, 1970.

Meynaud, Jean, *Social Change and Economic Development*, Paris, UNESCO, 1963.

Novack, D.E. and R. Lekachman (eds), *Development and Society: The Dynamics of Economic Change*, New York, St Martin's Press, 1964.

Pye, Lucian W., *Aspects of Political Development*, Boston, MA, Little, Brown, 1966.

Sinai, I. Robert, *The Challenge of Modernization: The West's Impact on the non-Western World*, New York, Norton, 1964.

Vajpeyi, Dhirendra K., *Modernization and Social Change in India*, New Delhi, Manohar, 1979.

Varma, Baidya Nath, *The Sociology and Politics of Development: A Theoretical Study*, London, Routledge and Kegan Paul, 1980.

Weiner, Myron (ed.), *Modernization: The Dynamics of Growth*, New York, Basic Books, 1966.

Development Theory

Adelman, Irma and Cynthia Taft Morris, *Economic Growth and Social Equity in Developing Countries*, Stanford, CA, Stanford University Press, 1973.

Amin, Samir, *Accumulation on a World Scale: Critique of the Theory of Underdevelopment*, New York, Monthly Review Press, 1974.

Bauer, P.T, *Dissent on Development: Studies and Debates in Development Economics*, Delhi, Vikas, 1973.

Bechtold, Karl-Heinz, "Theories of Regional Growth and Development Strategies: A Critical Survey," *Economics*, vol. 16, 1977, pp. 90–104.

Bhagwati, Jagdish, *The Economics of Underdeveloped Countries*, New York, McGraw Hill, 1966.

Bhatt, V.V., *Development Perspectives: Problems, Strategy and Policies*, Oxford, Pergamon Press, 1980.

————, "Economic Development: An Analytical–Historical Approach," *World Development*, vol. 4, no. 7, 1976, pp. 583–92.

Chenery, Hollis B. et al., *Redistribution with Growth*, London, Oxford University Press, 1974.

Chenery, Hollis B., *Structural Change and Development Policy*, Oxford, Oxford University Press, 1979.

Currie, Lauchlin, "The Objectives of Development," *World Development*, vol. 6, no. 1, 1978, pp. 1–10.

Dasgupta, Ajit K., *Economic Theory and the Developing Countries*, London, Macmillan, 1974.

Delbeke, Jos, "Recent Long-Wave Theories: A Critical Survey," *Futures*, vol. 13, no. 4, August 1981, pp. 246–57.

El-Shagi, E.S., "The Relevance of the Predominant Theories of Economic Integration for Development Strategy," *Economics*, vol. 17, 1978, pp. 71–109.

Frank, Andre Gunder, *Sociology of Development and Underdevelopment of Sociology*, London, Pluto Press, 1971.

Galtung, Johan and Anders Wirak, *Human Needs, Human Rights and the Theory of Development*, Oslo, University of Oslo Chair in Conflict and Peace Research, 1976.

Galtung, Johan, Roy Preiswerk and Monica Wemegh, "A Concept of Development Centred on the Human Being: Some Western European Perspectives," *Canadian Journal of Development Studies*, vol. 11, no. 1, 1981, pp. 134–63.

Galtung, Johan, Peter O'Brien and Roy Preiswerk (eds), *Self-Reliance: A Strategy for Development*, London, Bogle L'Ouverture, 1980.

Ghai, D.P. et al., *The Basic Needs Approach to Development: Some Issues Regarding Concept and Methodology*, Geneva, ILO, 1977.

Gianaris, Nicholas V., *Economic Development: Thoughts and Problems*, North Quincy, MA, Christopher, 1978.

Goulet, Denis, *The Cruel Choice: A New Concept in the Theory of Development*, New York, Atheneum, 1971.

Hettne, Bjorn, "Current Issues in Development Theory," *Sarec Report*, vol. 5, 1978, pp. 31–9.

Higgins, Benjamin, *Economic Development: Problems, Principles and Policies*, New York, Norton, 1968.

Hla Myint, U., *Economic Theory and the Underdeveloped Countries*, New York, Oxford University Press, 1971.

Hoselitz, Bert Frank (ed.), *Theories of Economic Growth*, New York, Free Press, 1960.

Huang, C.C. Philip (ed.), *The Development of Under-development in China: A Symposium*, New York, M.E. Sharpe, 1980.

ILO, *The Basic Needs Approach to Development*, Geneva, 1977.

Kitamura, Hiroshi, "Challenge of Development Economics: Relevance of Economic Theory to Contemporary Development Problems," *Developing Economies*, vol. 13, no. 1, March 1975, pp. 3–21.

Lehmann, David (ed.), *Development Theory: Four Critical Essays*, London, Frank Cass, 1979.

Livingstone, Ian, "The Development of Development Economics," *ODI Review*, vol. 2, 1981, pp. 1–19.

Mafeje, Archie (ed.), *Science, Ideology and Development: Three Essays on Development Theory*, Uppsala, Scandinavian Institute of African Studies, 1978.

Meier, Gerald M. and Robert E. Baldwin, *Economic Development: Theory, History, Policy*, New York, John Wiley, 1957.

Menck, K.W., A. Naini and A. Nottelmann, "Prospects of the World Models for the Third Development Decade," *Economics*, vol. 23, 1981, pp. 116–42.

Myint, H., *The Economics of Developing Countries*, London, Hutchinson University Library, 1973.

Myrdal, Gunnar, *Asian Drama: An Inquiry into the Poverty of Nations*, New York, Pantheon, 1968.

——, *Economic Theory and Underdeveloped Regions*, London, Duckworth, 1957.

Nisbet, Robert A., *Social Change and History: Aspects of the Western Theory of Development*, London, Oxford University Press, 1969.

Novack, David E. and Robert Lekachman (eds), *Development and Society; The Dynamics of Economic Change*, New York, St Martin's Press, 1964.

Owens, Edgar and Robert Shaw, *Development Reconsidered*, Lexington, MA, D.C. Heath, 1972.

Palma, G., "Dependency: A Formal Theory of Underdevelopment or a Methodology for the Analysis of Concrete Situations of Underdevelopment?," *World Development*, vol. 16, nos 7/8, July/August 1978, pp. 881–924.

Phillipps, A., "The Concept of 'Development' ," *Review of African Political Economy*, vol. 8, 1977.

Qureshi, M.L., *Approach to a New Development Strategy for Asian Countries*, Islamabad, Pakistan Institute of Development Economics, 1975.

Rimmer, Douglas, " 'Basic Needs' and the Origins of the Development Ethos," *Journal of Developing Areas*, vol. 15, no. 2, January 1981, pp. 215–38.

Rothstein, Robert L. "The Political Economy of Redistribution and Self-reliance," *World Development*, vol. 4, no. 7, 1976, pp. 593–611.

Sachs, Ignacy, "Gandhi and Development: A European View," in Johan Galtung, Peter O'Brien and Roy Preiswerk (eds), *Self-reliance: A Strategy for Development*, London, Bogle L'Ouverture, 1980, pp. 45-57.

Streeten, Paul P., "Development Ideas in Historical Perspective: The New Interest in Development," *Regional Development Dialogue*, vol. 1, no. 2, Autumn 1980, pp. 1–31.

Streeten, Paul and Shahid Javed Burki, "Basic Needs: Some Issues," *World Development*, vol. 6, no. 3, 1978, pp. 411–21.

Teune, Henry and Zdravko Mlinar, *The Concept of Development: Theory and Policy*, Vienna, Vienna Institute for Development, 1973.

Varma, Baidya Nath, *The Sociology and Politics of Development: A Theoretical Study*, London, Routledge and Kegan Paul, 1980.

Development, Equity and Freedom

Abdalla, Ismail-Sabri, "What Development? A Third World Viewpoint," *International Development Review*, vol. 22, nos 2/3, 1980, pp. 13–16.

Adelman, Irma, "Growth, Income Distribution and Equity Oriented Development Strategies," *World Development*, vol. 3, nos 2/3, Feb/March 1975, pp. 67–76.

Adelman, Irma and Cynthia Taft, *Economic Growth and Social Equity in Developing Countries*, Stanford, CA, Stanford University Press, 1973.

Amarshi, Azeem et al., *Development and Dependency: The Political Economy of Papua New Guinea*, Melbourne, Oxford University Press, 1979.

Amin, Samir, *Accumulation on a World Scale: Critique of the Theory of Underdevelopment*, New York, Monthly Review Press, 1974.

Bhatt, V.V., *Development Perspectives: Problems, Strategy and Policies*, Oxford, Pergamon Press, 1980.

Brown, Lester R., *The Interdependence of Nations*, New York, Foreign Policy, 1972.

Chenery, Hollis B. et al., *Redistribution with Growth: Policies to Improve Income Distribution in Developing Countries in the Context of Economic Growth*—A Joint Study by the World Bank's Development Research Center and the Institute of Development Studies, University of Sussex, London, Oxford University Press, 1974.

Chenery, Hollis B., "Restructuring the World Economy," *Foreign Affairs*, vol. 53, no. 2, January 1975, pp. 242–63.

————, *Structural Change and Development Policy*, Washington, D.C., International Bank for Reconstruction and Development, 1979.

Chenery, Hollis B. and M. Syrquin, *Patterns of Development, 1950–1970*, London, Oxford University Press, 1975.

Chenery, Hollis B. et al., *Towards a Strategy for Development Co-operation, with Special Reference to Asia*, Rotterdam, Universitaire pers Rotterdam, 1967.

De Kadt, Emanuel, "Some Basic Questions on Human Rights and Development," *World Development*, vol. 8, no. 2, Feb 1980, pp. 97–105.

Development Choices for the 1980s and Beyond [papers presented at the 16th World Conference of the Society for International Development, Colombo, Aug. 13–15, 1979], *International Development Review*, vol. 22, nos 2/3, 1980, pp. 3–125.

Erb, Guy F. and Valeriana Kallab, *Beyond Dependency: The Developing World Speaks Out*, Washington, D.C., Overseas Development Council, 1975.

Fields, Gary S., *Poverty, Inequality and Development*, London, Cambridge University Press, 1980.

Frank, Charles R. and R.C. Webb, *Income Distribution and Growth in the Less-developed Countries*, Washington, D.C., Brookings Institution, 1977.

Galtung, Johan, "Self-reliance: Concepts, Practice and Rationale," in Johan Galtung, Peter O'Brien and Roy Preiswerk (eds), *Self-Reliance: A Strategy for Development*, London, Bogle-L'Ouverture Pub. Ltd., 1980, pp. 19–44.

Galtung, Johan and Anders Wirak, *Human Needs, Human Rights and the Theory of Development*, Oslo, University of Oslo, Chair in Conflict and Peace Research, 1976.

Gregory, Mary et al., "Poverty, Income Distribution and Development Strategies for India," *ODI Review*, vol. 2, 1979, pp. 23–40.

Hicks, Norman, *Economic Growth and Human Resources*, Washington, D.C., World Bank, 1980.

Irvine, John, "The Choice of Ways of Life in the North – and the Scope for Southern Intervention," *International Development Review*, vol. 22, nos. 2/3, 1980, pp. 55–66.

Khan, A.R., *Growth and Inequality in the Rural Philippines*, Geneva, ILO, 1976.

Parmar, Samuel, L., "Self-reliant Development in an 'Interdependent' World," in Guy F. Erb and Valeriana Kallab (eds), *Beyond Dependency: The Developing World Speaks Out*, Washington, D.C., Overseas Development Council, 1975, pp. 3–27.

Rist, Gilbert, "Alternative Strategies to Development," *International Development Review*, vol. 22, nos. 2/3, 1980, pp. 102–15.

Rondinelli, Dennis A., "National Investment Planning and Equity Policy in Developing Countries: The Challenge of Decentralized Administration," *Policy Sciences*, vol. 10, no. 1, August 1978, pp. 45–74.

Sen, Amartya, *An Economic Inequality*, Oxford, Clarendon Press, 1978.

Soedjatmoko, *Development and Freedom*, Tokyo, Simul Press, 1979.

Streeten, Paul, "The Choices Before Us," *International Development Review*, vol. 22, nos 2/3, 1980, pp. 3–11.

Uri, Pierre, *Development Without Dependence*, New York, Praeger, 1976.

World Bank, *Employment and Income Distribution in Indonesia*, Washington, D.C., 1979.

Basic Needs and Human Development

Adelman, Irma, Cynthia T. Morris and Sherman Robinson, "Policies for Equitable Growth," *World Development*, vol. 4, no. 7, 1976, pp. 561–82.

Ahluwalia, Montek S. et al., *Growth and Poverty in Developing Countries*, Washington, D.C., World Bank, 1979.

Banskota, M., *Basic Needs: An Alternative Development Strategy for Nepal*, Kathmandu, Centre for Economic Development and Administration, 1979.

Beg, M.A.K. et al., *Basic Needs and Rural Development*, Peshawar, Pakistan Academy of Rural Development, 1980. (International Seminar on Basic Needs Strategy for Rural Development, Peshawar, May 1979.)

Birdsall, Nancy, *Population and Poverty in the Developing World*, Washington, D.C., World Bank, 1980.

Blaikie, M.P. et al., *The Struggle for Basic Needs in Nepal*, Paris, Organisation for Economic Cooperation and Development, 1979.

Burki, Shahid Javed, "Meeting Basic Needs: An Overview," *World Development*, vol. 9, no. 2, February 1981, pp. 167–82.

Chong Kee Park, *Development Programs and Strategies for Meeting Basic Human Needs and Raising Incomes and Standards of Living with Emphasis on Rural Areas*, Seoul, Korea Development Institute, 1978.

Churchill, Anthony A. et al., *Shelter*, Washington, D.C., World Bank, 1980.

Conde, J., M.J. Paraiso and V.K. Ayassou, *The Integrated Approach to Rural Development, Health and Population*, Paris, Organisation for Economic Co-operation and Development, 1979.

Ensminger, Douglas and Paul Boman, *Conquest of World Hunger and Poverty*, Ames, Iowa, The Iowa State University Press, 1980.

Esman, Milton J., *The Administration of Human Development*, Washington, D.C., World Bank, 1980.

Ghai, D.P. et al., *The Basic-needs Approach to Development; Some Issues Regarding Concepts and Methodology*, Geneva, ILO, 1977.

Haq, Mahbub Ul, *The Poverty Curtain: Choices for the Third World*, New York, Columbia University Press, 1976.

Haq, Mahbub Ul and S.J. Burki, *Meeting Basic Needs: An Overview*, Washington, D.C., World Bank, 1980.

Higgins, B., "The Disenthronement of Basic Needs? Twenty Questions," *Regional Development Dialogue*, vol. 1, 1980, pp. 79–116.

Heyneman, Stephen P., *Investment in Indian Education: Uneconomic?* Washington, D.C., World Bank, 1979.

ILO, *Employment, Growth and Basic Needs: A One World Problem*, Geneva, 1976.

————, *Meeting Basic Needs; Strategies for Eradicating Mass Poverty and Unemployment: Conclusions of the World Employment Conference 1976*, Geneva, 1976.

————, *Poverty and Employment in Rural Areas of the Developing Countries*, Geneva, 1979.

————, *Poverty and Landlessness in Rural Asia*, Geneva, 1977.

————, *Profiles of Rural Poverty*, Geneva, 1979.

King, Timothy (ed.),   *Education and Income*, Washington, D.C., World Bank, 1980.

Lisk, F.,   "Conventional Development Strategies and Basic Needs Fulfilment," *International Labour Review*, vol. 115, 1977, pp. 175–91.

McGinn, Noel F. et al.,   *Education and Development in Korea*, Cambridge, MA, Council on East Asian Studies, 1980.

Meesook, O.A.,   "Contribution of Human Resources to Economic Growth," in Vinyu Vichit-Vadakan and Padma Mallampally (eds), *Readings in Development and Planning*, Bangkok, UN Asian and Pacific Development Institute, 1979; 104–25.

Mehmet, Ozay (ed.),   *Poverty and Social Change in Southeast Asia*, Ottawa, University of Ottawa Press, 1979.

Morawetz, D.,   "Basic Needs Policies and Population Growth," *World Development*, vol. 6, 1978, pp. 1251–59.

Murdoch, William W.,   *The Poverty of Nations: The Political Economy of Hunger and Population*, Baltimore, Johns Hopkins University Press, 1980.

Nagamine, H.,   *Study on Planning for Basic Needs*, A paper presented to the Workshop on improving the methods of planning for comprehensive regional development, United Nations Centre for Regional Development, Nagoya, 1978.

Noor, Abdun,   *Education and Basic Human Needs*, Washington, D.C., 1981.

Planning for Basic Needs and Mobilization of Resources, Report of a National Seminar, Bangkok, Asian Employment Programme, 1980.

"Poverty and Inequality," *World Development*, vol. 6, no. 3, March 1978, pp. 241–421.

Proceedings of the Seminar on Development of Basic Community Services Through Primary Health Care, Bangkok, 10 Oct.–24 Nov. 1978, Bangkok, UN Asian and Pacific Development Institute, 1978.

Report of the Symposium on Changes in Food Habits in Relation to Increase of Productivity, Manila, 22–28 Aug. 1972, Tokyo, Asian Productivity Organization, 1973.

Reutlinger, Shlomo and M. Selowsky,   *Malnutrition and Poverty: Magnitude and Policy Options*, Baltimore, Johns Hopkins University Press, 1976.

Richards, Peter and Wilbert Gooneratne,   *Basic Needs, Poverty and Government Policies in Sri Lanka*, Geneva, ILO, 1980.

Rimmer, Douglas,   " 'Basic Needs' and the Origins of the Development Ethos," *Journal of Developing Areas*, vol. 15, no. 2, January 1981, pp. 215–38.

Rudra, A.,   *The Basic Needs Concept and its Implication in Indian Development Planning*, Bangkok, ILO-ARTEP, 1978.

Sen, Amartya,   *Levels of Poverty: Policy and Change*, Washington, D.C., World Bank, 1980.

Soedjatmoko,   "National Policy Implications of the Basic Needs Model," *Prisma*, vol. 9, 1978, pp. 3–25.

Srinivasan, T.N.,   "Malnutrition: Some Measurement and Issues," *Journal of Development Economics*, vol. 8, no. 1, February 1981, pp. 3–19.

Standing, Guy and Richard Szal, *Poverty and Basic Needs: Evidence from Guyana and the Philippines*, Geneva, ILO, 1979.

Streeten, Paul and Shahid Javed Burki, "Basic Needs: Some Issues," *World Development*, vol. 6, no. 3, 1978, pp. 411–21.

Visaria, Pravin, *Poverty and Unemployment in India: An Analysis of Recent Evidence*, Washington, D.C., World Bank, 1980.

Wheeler, D., "Basic Needs Fulfillment and Economic Growth," *Journal of Development Economics*, vol. 7, 1980, pp. 435–51.

World Bank, *Aspects of Poverty in the Philippines: A Review and Assessment*, Washington, D.C., 1980.

————, *Assault on World Poverty: Problems of Rural Development, Education and Health*, Baltimore, Johns Hopkins University Press, 1975.

————, *Health: Sector Policy Paper*, Washington, D.C., 1980.

————, *Malaysia: Selected Issues in Rural Poverty*, Washington, D.C., 1980.

————, *Meeting Basic Needs: An Overview*, Washington, D.C., 1980.

————, *Nutrition and Health of Indonesian Construction Workers: Endurance and Anemia*, Washington, D.C., 1973.

————, *Poverty and Basic Needs*, Washington, D.C., 1980.

————, *Poverty and the Development of Human Resources: Regional Perspectives*, Washington, D.C., 1980.

————, *The Relationship of Nutrition and Health to Worker Productivity in Kenya*, Washington, D.C., 1977.

Zukin, Paul, Health and Economic Development: How Significant is the Relationship? *International Development*, vol. 17, no. 2, 1975, pp. 17–21.

Poverty

Adelman, Irma, Cynthia Taft Morris and Sherman Robinson, "Policies for Equitable Growth," *World Development*, vol. 4, no. 7, pp. 561–82.

Ahluwalia, Montek S. et al., *Growth and Poverty in Developing Countries*, Washington, D.C., World Bank, 1979.

Balakrishnan, S. and Pralay K. Ghosh, "Poverty Line Re-defined and Confirmed," *Behavioural Sciences and Rural Development*, vol. 3, no. 1, January 1980, pp. 1–9.

Bhagwati, Jagdish, *The Economics of Underdeveloped Countries*, New York, McGraw Hill, 1966.

Birdsall, Nancy, *Population and Poverty in the Developing World*, Washington, D.C., World Bank, 1980.

Chambers, Robert, *Rural Poverty Unperceived: Problems and Remedies*, Washington, D.C., World Bank, 1980.

Dandekar, V.M. and Nilakantha Rath, *Poverty in India*, Poona, Indian School of Political Economy, 1971.

Elliot, Charles, *Patterns of Poverty in the Third World: A Study of Social and Economic Stratification*, New York, Praeger, 1975.

Ensminger, Douglas and Paul Boman, *Conquest of World Hunger and Poverty*, Ames, Iowa, The Iowa State University Press, 1980.

Fields, Gary S., *Poverty, Inequality and Development*, Cambridge, Cambridge University Press, 1980.

Frank, André Gunder, *Sociology of Development and Underdevelopment of Sociology*, London, Pluto Press, 1971.

Galbraith, John Kenneth, *The Nature of Mass Poverty*, Harmondsworth, Penguin, 1980.

Griffin, Keith, "Growth and Impoverishment in the Rural Areas of Asia," *World Development*, vol. 7, nos 4/5, April–May 1979, pp. 361–83.

Hainsworth, Geoffrey B., "Economic Growth and Poverty in Southeast Asia: Malaysia, Indonesia and the Philippines," *Pacific Affairs*, vol. 52, no. 1, Spring 1979, pp. 5–41.

Haq, Mahbub Ul, *The Poverty Curtain: Choices for the Third World*, New York, Columbia University Press, 1976.

Harrison, Paul, *Inside the Third World: The Anatomy of Poverty*, Harmondsworth, Penguin, 1981.

Hayter, Teresa, *The Creation of World Poverty: An Alternative View to the Brandt Report*, London, Pluto Press, 1981.

ILO, *Poverty and Landlessness in Rural Asia*, Geneva, 1977.

————, *Profiles of Rural Poverty*, Geneva, 1979.

James, Dorothy Buckton (ed.), *Analyzing Poverty Policy*, Lexington, Lexington Books, 1975.

Kakwani, Nanak C., *Income Inequality and Poverty: Methods of Estimation and Policy Application*, New York, Oxford University Press, 1980.

Kim, Do Hyung, "Expenditure Distribution and Patterns of the Poor in Korea," *The Developing Economies*, vol. 19, no. 1, March 1981, pp. 17–38.

Mathur, Hari Mohan, "Ending Poverty, Unemployment and Inequality: Experiences and Strategy," *Development Policy and Administration Review*, vol. 1, no. 2, July/December 1975.

Meesook, Dey Astra, *Income, Consumption and Poverty in Thailand, 1962/63 to 1975/76*, Washington, D.C., World Bank, 1979.

Mehmet, Ozay (ed.), *Poverty and Social Change in Southeast Asia*, Ottawa, University of Ottawa Press, 1979.

Murdoch, William W., *The Poverty of Nations: The Political Economy of Hunger and Population*, Baltimore, Johns Hopkins University Press, 1980.

Myrdal, Gunnar, *Asian Drama: An Inquiry into the Poverty of Nations*, New York, Pantheon, 1968.

Peacock, Frank, "Rural Poverty and Development in West Malaysia [1957–1970]," *Journal of Developing Areas*, vol. 15, no. 4, July 1981, pp. 639–54.

"Poverty and Inequality," *World Development*, vol. 6, no. 3, March 1978, pp. 241–421.

Rao, V.V. Bhanoji, "Measurement of Deprivation and Poverty Based on the Proportion Spent on Food: An Exploratory Exercise," *World Development*, vol. 9, no. 4, 1981, pp. 337–53.

Richards, Peter and Wilbert Gooneratne, *Basic Needs, Poverty and Government Policies in Sri Lanka*, Geneva, ILO, 1980.

Rodgers, G.B. "A Conceptualisation of Poverty in Rural India," *World Development*, vol. 4, no. 4, 1976, pp. 261–76.

Schuttz, Theodore W., "Nobel Lecture: The Economics of Being Poor," *Journal of Political Economy*, vol. 88, no. 41, 1980, pp. 639–51.

Scott, Wolf, *Concepts and Measurement of Poverty*, Geneva, United Nations Research Institute for Social Development, 1981.

Seminar on Planning for Basic Needs and Mobilization of Resources, Kathmandu, 12–14 November 1979, Bangkok, ARTEP, 1980.

Sen, Amartya, *Levels of Poverty: Policy and Change*, Washington, D.C., World Bank, 1980.

Standing, Guy and Richard Szal, *Poverty and Basic Needs: Evidence from Guyana and the Philippines*, Geneva, ILO, 1979.

Symposium on New Directions of Asia's Development Strategies, Tokyo, March 13–16, 1979, Proceedings and papers, Tokyo, Institute of Development Economies, 1980.

UN Asian and Pacific Development Institute, *Local Level Planning and Rural Development: Alternative Strategies*, New Delhi, Concept Publishing Company, 1980.

Visaria, Pravin, *Poverty and Unemployment in India: An Analysis of Recent Evidence*, Washington, D.C., World Bank, 1980.

World Bank, *Aspects of Poverty in the Philippines: A Review and Assessment*, Washington, D.C., 1980.

————, *Malaysia: Selected Issues on Rural Poverty*, Washington, D.C., 1980.

————, *Poverty and Basic Needs*, Washington, D.C., 1980.

————, *Poverty and the Development of Human Resources: Regional Perspectives*, Washington, D.C., 1980.

Managing the Outer Limits to Growth

Brown, Lester R., *Building a Sustainable Society*, New York, W.W. Norton, 1981.

————, *The Global Economic Prospect: New Sources of Economic Stress*, Washington, D.C., Worldwatch Institute, 1978.

————, *In the Human Interest: A Strategy to Stabilize World Population*, Oxford, Pergamon Press, 1976.

————, *Man and His Environment: Food*, New York, Harper and Row, 1972.

————, *Resource Trends and Population Policy: A Time for Reassessment*, Washington, D.C., Worldwatch Institute, 1979.

————, *Twenty-two Dimensions of the Population Problem*, Washington, D.C., Department of Medical and Public Affairs, The George Washington University Medical Center, 1976.

————, *The Worldwide Loss of Cropland*, Washington, D.C., Worldwatch Institute, 1978.

Brown, Lester R. and Erik P. Eckholm, *By Bread Alone*, New York, Praeger, 1974.

Dorner, Peter and Mahmoud A. El-Shafie, *Resources and Development: Natural Resource Policies and Economic Development in an Interdependent World*, London, Croom Helm, 1980.

Eckholm, Erik, *Planting for the Future: Forestry for Human Needs*, Washington, D.C., Worldwatch Institute, 1979.

————, *The Other Energy Crisis: Firewood*, Washington, D.C., Worldwatch Institute, 1975.

The Global 2000 Report to the President, A report prepared by the Council on Environmental Quality and the Department of State, Washington, D.C., 1981.

Hueting, Roefie, *New Scarcity and Economic Growth: More Welfare Through Less Production?* Amsterdam, North-Holland, 1980.

Laszlo, Ervin (ed.), *Goals for Mankind: A Report to the Club of Rome*, London, Hutchinson, 1977.

Leontief, Wassily, Ann P. Carter and Peter A. Petri, *The Future of the World Economy: A United Nations Study*, New York, Oxford University Press, 1977.

Matthews, William H. (ed.), *Outer Limits and Human Needs: Resources and Environmental Issues of Development Strategies*, Uppsala, Dag Hammarskjold Foundation, 1976.

McNamara, Robert S., *One Hundred Countries, Two Billion People: The Dimensions of Development*, New York, Praeger, 1973.

Meadows, Donella H. et al., *The Limits to Growth: A Report for the Club of Rome's Project on the Predicament of Mankind*, New York, Universe Books, 1974.

Mesarovic, Mihajlo and Eduard Pestel, *Mankind at the Turning Point: The Second Report to the Club of Rome*, New York, E.P. Dutton, 1974.

Peccei, Aurelio, "The Responsibility of the Developed Countries," *International Development Review*, vol. 22, nos. 2/3, 1980, pp. 75–79.

Pearson, Lester B., *Partners in Development: Report of the Commission on International Development*, New York, Praeger, 1969.

Ruster, Bernd et al. (eds), *International Protection of the Environment: Treaties and Related Documents*, New York, Oceana, 1981.

Sachs, Ignacy, *Foreign Trade and Economic Development of Underdeveloped Countries*, New York, Asia Publishing House, 1965.

————, *Studies in Political Economy of Development*, New York, Pergamon, 1980.

Scanning our Future: A Report from NGO Forum on the World Economic Order in Support of the Seventh Special Session of the UN General Assembly on Development and International Economic Co-operation [Sept. 1–12, 1975], New York, Carnegie Endowment for International Peace, 1975.

Schmalz, Anton B. (ed.), *Today's Choices Tomorrow's Opportunities*, Washington, D.C., World Future Society, 1974.

Singh, Jyoti Shankar, *A New International Economic Order: Towards a Fair Redistribution of the World's Resources*, New York, Praeger, 1977.

Spekke, Andrew A. (ed.), *The Next 25 Years: Crisis and Opportunity*, Washington, D.C., World Future Society, 1975.

Tinbergen, Jan et al., *Reshaping the International Order: A Report to the Club of Rome*, New York, Dutton, 1976.

United Nations, *Interrelations: Resources, Environment, Population and Development: Proceedings of a U.N. Symposium Held at Stockholm from 6–10 Aug. 1979*, New York, 1980.

————, *Report of Habitat: UN Conference on Human Settlements*, Vancouver, May 31–June 11, 1976, New York, 1977.

————, *Report of the World Food Conference, August, 1974*, New York, 1975.

————, Institute for Training and Research. *International Cooperation for Pollution Control*, New York, 1973.

Ward, Barbara, *The Home of Man*, New York, 1976.

Ward, Barbara and Rene Dubos, *Only One Earth*, New York, Ballantine Books, 1973.

What Now: Another Development, The 1975 Dag Hammarskjold Report on development and international cooperation prepared on the occasion of the Seventh Special Session of the United Nations General Assembly, Uppsala, Dag Hammarskjold Foundation, 1975.

Planning for Food and Energy

Ad Hoc Advisory Group Meeting on Special Study on Food Supply in the ESCAP Region, Bangkok, 19–20 January, 1981, *Note on the Proposed Special Study on Food Supply in the ESCAP Region* [*and the report*], Bangkok, 1981.

Aziz, Sartaj (ed.), *Hunger, Politics and Markets; The Real Issues in the Food Crisis*, New York, New York University Press, 1975.

Brown, Lester R., *Food or Fuel: New Competition for the World's Cropland*, Washington, D.C., Worldwatch Institute, 1980.

————, "Global Food Insecurity," *Futurist*, vol. 8, no. 2, April 1974, pp. 56–64.

————, *Increasing World Food Output: Problems and Prospects*, Washington, D.C., US Department of Agriculture, 1965.

————, *Man, Land and Food: Looking Ahead at World Food Needs*, Washington, D.C., US Department of Agriculture, 1963.

————, *Our Daily Bread*, New York, Foreign Policy, 1975.

————, "Toward a World Bank: Dealing with the World's Food Security," *Current*, vol. 154, 1973, pp. 53–61.

————, *The Worldwide Loss of Cropland*, Washington, D.C., Worldwatch Institute, 1978.

Campbell, Keith O, *Food for the Future: How Agriculture can Meet the Challenge*, London, University of Nebraska Press, 1979.

Chin, H.F., et al. (eds), *Food and Agriculture Malaysia 2000*, Serdang, Faculty of Agriculture, Universiti Pertanian Malaysia, 1978.

Christensen, Cheryl, *The Right to Food: How to Guarantee*, New York, Institute for World Order, 1978.

Dandekar, V.M., *Crop Insurance for Developing Countries*, New York, Agricultural Development Council, 1977.

————, *Food and Freedom*, Dharwar, Karnatak University, 1967.

————, *Use of Food Surpluses for Economic Development*, Poona, Gokhale Institute, 1956.

Dumont, Rene and Nicholas Cohen, *The Growth of Hunger: A New Politics of Agriculture*, London, Marion Boyars, 1980.

Eckholm, Erik P., *Losing Ground: Environmental Stress and World Food Prospects*, New York, W.W. Norton, 1976.

Fallen-Bailey, D.G. and T.A. Byer, *Energy Options and Policy Issues in Developing Countries: A Background Study for World Development Report 1979*, Washington, D.C., International Bank for Reconstruction and Development, 1979.

Food and Agriculture Organization of the United Nations, *The Struggle for Food Security*, Rome, 1979.

Frederick, K.D., "Energy Use and Agricultural Production in Developing Countries," in R.G. Ridker (ed.), *Changing Resource Problems of the Fourth World*, Washington, D.C., Resources for the Future, 1976.

Global Food Assessment, 1980, Washington, D.C., International Economics Division, US Department of Agriculture, 1980.

Hayes, Denis, *Energy for Development: Third World Options*, Washington, D.C., Worldwatch Institute, 1977.

Heichel, G.H., "Agricultural Production and Energy Resources," *American Scientist*, vol. 64, 1976, pp. 64–72.

Hoeft, R.G. and Siemens, J.C., "Do Fertilizers Waste Energy?" *Crops and Soil*, vol. 11, pp. 12–14.

Huddleston, Barbara and Jon McLin, *Political Investments in Food Production*, Bloomington, Indiana University Press, 1979.

International Symposium on Energy Strategies for Subsistence Agriculture, Mexico City, June 28 – July 1st, 1981, Mexico City, International Institute for Environment and Development, 1981.

Jones, David, *Food and Interdependence: The Effect of Food and Agricultural Policies of Developed Countries on the Food Problems of Developing Countries*, London, Overseas Development Institute, 1976.

Joseph, Raymond A., "Rising Oil Prices Spur the Third World to Convert its Sugar Surpluses into Fuel," *Wall Street Journal*, 10 July, 1979.

Ker, A.D.R., *Food or Famine: An Account of the Crop Science Programme Supported by the International Development Research Centre*, Ottawa, International Development Research Centre, 1979.

Knudsen, Odin and Pasquale L. Scandizzo, *Nutrition and Food Needs in Developing Countries*, Washington, D.C., International Bank for Reconstruction and Development, 1979.

Lappe, Frances Moore and Joseph Collins, *Food First; Beyond the Myth of Scarcity*, Rev. ed. New York, Ballantine Books, 1978.

Leach, G., *Energy and Food Production*, Guildford, Surrey, IPC Science and Technology Press, 1976.

Makhijani, Arjun, *Energy Policy for the Rural Third World*, London, International Institute for Environment Development, 1976.

Mayer, Jean et al., *Food and Nutrition Policy in Changing World*, New York, Oxford University Press, 1979.

Meador, Roy, *Future Energy Alternatives: Long-range Energy Prospects for America and the World*, Ann Arbor, Michigan, Ann Arbor Science, 1979.

Muhammad, Ali, *Study on Food Production: Tentative Outline of Study*, New Delhi, 1980.

Nathan, Richard A., *Fuels from Sugar Crops*, Washington, D.C., Battelle Institute for the US Department of Energy, 1978.

Organization of Arab Petroleum Exporting Countries, *Energy Developments: Consumption, Policies, Sources*, Kuwait, 1979.

Ortamier, E., "The Production of Ethanol from Sugar Cane: Brazil's Experiment for a Partial Solution to the Energy Problem," *Quarterly Journal of International Agriculture*, vol. 20, no. 3, July–September 1981.

Paarlberg, Don, "A World Food Policy that can Succeed," *Futurist*, vol. 9, no. 6, December 1975, pp. 300–02.

Palmedo, Philip F. et al., *Energy Needs, Uses and Resources in Developing Countries*, New York, Policy Analysis Division, National Centre for Analysis of Energy Systems, Brookhaven National Laboratory, 1978.

Pimentel, D. and E.C. Terhune, "Energy Use in Food Production," in E.R. Duncan (ed.), *Dimensions of World Food Problems*, Ames, Iowa State University Press, 1977.

Pimental, D. et al., "Food Production and the Energy Crisis," *Science*, vol. 182, October 1973, pp. 4110.

Price, Donald R., "Fuel, Food and the Future," in Marylin Chou and David P. Harmon (eds), *Critical Food Issues of the Eighties*, New York, Pergamon Press, 1979, pp. 234–44.

Reutlinger, Shlomo, *Food Security in Food Deficit Countries*, Washington, D.C., International Bank for Reconstruction and Development, 1980.

Slesser, M., "Energy and Food," in N.S. Scrimshaw and M. Behar (eds), *Nutrition and Agricultural Development*, New York, Plenum Press, 1976.

——, "Energy Subsidy as a Criterion in Food Policy Planning," *Journal of Science of Food Agriculture*, vol. 24, 1973.

Smil, V. and W.E. Knowland (eds), *Energy in the Developing World: The Real Energy Crisis*, New York, Oxford University Press, 1980.

Soedjatmoko, *Turning Point in Development: The Food-Energy Pivot*, Tokyo, United Nations University, 1981.

Steinhart, J.S. and C.E. Steinhart, "Energy Use in the U.S. Food System," in P.H. Abelson (ed.), *Food: Politics, Economics, Nutrition and Research*, Washington, D.C., American Association for the Advancement of Science, 1975.

Sudarmadji, S., "Food Consumption and Production Problems in ASEAN," *Kajian Ekonomi Malaysia*, vol. 16, nos 1/2, June–December 1979, pp. 388–97.

Tyers, Rodney (ed.), *Food Security in Asia and the Pacific: Issues for Research*, Honolulu, East-West Resource Systems Institute, 1979.

United Nations Conference on Trade and Development, *Energy Supplies for Developing Countries: Issues in Transfer and Development of Technologies*, New York, 1980.

United States, Department of Agriculture, Economic Research Service, *The World Food Situation and Prospects to 1985*, Washington, D.C., 1974.

Workshop on Alternative Energy Strategies, *Energy: Global Prospects 1985–2000, Report of the Workshop*, New York, McGraw-Hill Co., 1977.

Role of Discrimination in Development Policy

Abramson, Joan, *The Invisible Women: Discrimination in the Academic Profession*, San Francisco, Jossey-Bass, 1975.

Alvarez, Rodolfo, *Discrimination in Organization: Using Social Indicators to Manage Social Change*, San Francisco, Jossey-Bass, 1980.

Beck, E.M. et al., "Industrial Segmentation and Labour Market Discrimination," *Social Problems*, vol. 28, December 1980, pp. 113–30.

Becker, Gary S., *Economics of Discrimination*, Rev. 2nd ed. Chicago, University of Chicago Press, 1971.

Beneria, Lourdes, "Reproduction, Production and the Sexual Division of Labour," *Cambridge Journal of Economics*, vol. 3, no. 3, September 1979, pp. 203–25.

Biddle, Richard E., *Discrimination: What Does it Mean?* Washington, D.C., International Personnel Management Association, 1973.

Bunzel, J.H., "Affirmative Action, Negative Results," *Encounter*, vol. 53, November 1979, pp. 43–51.

Chen, Lincoln et al., "Sex Bias in the Family: Allocation of Food and Health

Care in Rural Bangladesh," *Population and Development Review*, vol. 7, no. 1, March 1981, pp. 55–70.

Davin, Delia, *Women-work: Women and the Party in Revolutionary China*, Oxford, Oxford University Press, 1979.

Ekelund, R.B. et al., "Can Discrimination Increase Employment: a Neo-classical Perspective," *Southern Economic Journal*, vol. 47, January 1981, pp. 664–73.

Eley, Lynn W. and Thomas W. Casstevens., *The Politics of Fair-housing Legislation; State and Local Case Studies*, San Francisco, Chandler Publishers, 1968.

Fellows, B.J., *The Discrimination Process and Development*, New York, Pergamon, 1968.

Figueira-McDonough, J., "Discrimination in Social Work: Evidence, Myth and Ignorance," *Social Work*, 24 May, 1979, pp. 214–23.

Ford Foundation, *Women in the World*, New York, 1980.

Fried, Morton H. (ed.), *Systems of Equality and Inequality in Human Society*, New York, J.F. Bergin, 1981.

Furstenberg, George (ed.), *Patterns of Racial Discrimination*, Lexington, D.C. Heath, 1977.

Futehally, Laeeq (ed.), *Women in the Third World*, Bombay, Jaico Publishing House, 1980.

Jones, James E., " 'Reverse discrimination' in Employment: Judicial Treatment of Affirmative Action Programmes in the United States," *International Labour Review*, vol. 120, no. 4, July–August 1981, pp. 453–72.

Lockard, Duane, *Toward Equal Opportunity: A Study of State and Local Antidiscrimination Laws*, London, Macmillan, 1968.

Marshall, Ray, "The Economics of Racial Discrimination: A Survey," *Journal of Economic Literature*, vol. 12, no. 3, September 1974, pp. 849–71.

————, *Employment Discrimination: The Impact of Legal and Administrative Remedies*, New York, Praeger, 1978.

Okun, Arthur M., *Equality and Efficiency: The Big Tradeoff*, Washington, D.C., Brookings Institution, 1975.

Rogers, Barbara, *The Domestication of Women: Discrimination in Developing Societies*, New York, St. Martins Press, 1979.

Rowbotham, Sheila, *Women's Consciousness, Man's World*, Harmondsworth, Penguin, 1973.

Schiller, Bradley R., *The Economics of Poverty and Discrimination* (2nd ed.) Englewood Cliffs, Prentice-Hall, 1976.

Scott, Hilda, *Does Socialism Liberate Women? Experiences from Eastern Europe*, Boston, Beacon Press, 1974.

Semyonov, M., "Social Context of Women's Labour Force Participation: A Comparative Analysis," *American Journal of Sociology*, vol. 86, November 1980, pp. 534–50.

Sipila, Helvi, *The State of The World's Women 1979*, Oxfordshire, New International Publications Cooperative, 1979.

Sobhan, Salma, *Legal Status of Women in Bangladesh*, Dacca, Bangladesh Institute of Law and International Affairs, 1978.

Stimpson, Catherine R. (ed.), *Discrimination Against Women*, New York, Bowker, 1973.

United Nations General Assembly, *Equality Between Men and Women and*

Elimination of Discrimination Against Women, New York, 1976 [United Nations General Assembly Resolution 35 21 (XXX) 15 December].

Young, Jared J., *Discrimination Income, Human Capital Investment, and Asian-Americans*, Palo Alto, CA, R & E Research Associates, 1977.

Politicization and Conscientization as Prerequisites to Development

Bharadwaj, R., D.V. Ramana and V.N. Vinogradov, "Community Conscientization for Local Development," in Vinyu Vichit-Vadakan and A.I. Rogov (eds), *Environment (Resources) Management and Development*, Bangkok, UN Asian and Pacific Development Institute, 1980, pp. 410–25.

Bhasin, Kamla, *Breaking Barriers: A South Asian Experience of Training for Participatory Development*, Report of the Freedom-from-Hunger Campaign. Bangkok, FAO Regional Office for Asia, 1978.

Brandt, Vincent S., "The New Community Movement: Planned and Unplanned Change in Rural Korea," *Journal of Asian and African Studies*, vol. 13, nos 3/4, July–October 1978, pp. 196–211.

Carbonell, Aurora A., *The Role of Citizen Participation in Development*, Manila, College of Public Administration, University of the Philippines, 1976.

Cheema, G. Shabbir et al., *Rural Organisations and Rural Development in Selected Malaysian Villages*, Kuala Lumpur, UN Asian and Pacific Development Administration Centre, 1977.

Chitrakar, Jagadish K., *The Role of Panchayat in Nepal's Development*, Madison, Wisconsin, Center for Development, University of Wisconsin, 1977.

Coombs, Philip Hall and M. Ahmed, *Attacking Rural Poverty: How Nonformal Education Can Help*, Baltimore, Johns Hopkins University Press, 1974.

Cohen, John M. and Norman T. Uphoff, "Participation's Place in Rural Development: Seeking Clarity Through Specificity," *World Development*, vol. 8, no. 3, 1980, pp. 213–35.

Danforth, Devaratnam, "Citizen Participation in Community Development Through Local Government in Sri Lanka," *Planning and Administration*, vol. 5, no. 1, Spring 1978, pp. 41–52.

Dube, S.C., *India's Changing Villages: Human Factors in Community Development*, London, Routledge and Kegan Paul, 1958.

Dynamics of Nation-building, with Particular Reference to the Role of Communication, Report of the UNESCO Meeting, Kuala Lumpur, 14–28 September, 1979, Bangkok, Regional Office for Education in Asia and Oceania, Unesco, 1980.

Economic Commission for Africa, *Development Education: Rural Development Through Mass Media*, New York, United Nations, 1974.

ESCAP, *Role of Local Governments Co-operatives and Voluntary Agencies in Community Development*, Bangkok, 1973.

Food and Agriculture Organization of the United Nations, *Farmer's Organizations; Their Role in Community Development*, Rome, 1967.

Haq, M. Nurul, *The Role of People's Organization to Involve the Poor: A Country-Study on Bangladesh*, Bogra, Rural Development Academy, 1978.

Hossain, Mahabub, Raisul A. Mahmood and Qazi K. Ahmad, *'Participatory' Development Efforts in Rural Bangladesh – A Case Study of Experiences in Three Areas*, Geneva, ILO, 1979.

ILO, *Human Resources Development in Rural Areas in Asia and the Role of Rural Institutions: Education, Training and Institutions for Rural Human Resources Development in Asian Countries*, Geneva, 1975.

————, *Rural Employer's and Workers' Organisations and Participation*, Geneva, 1979.

Inayatullah (ed.), *Rural Organizations and Rural Development: Some Asian Experiences*, Kuala Lumpur, UN Asian and Pacific Development Administration Centre, 1977.

Knall, Bruno, "People's Participation in Development," *Local Government and Rural Development*, vol. 1, no. 2, April–June 1979, pp. 88–98.

Landsberger, Henry A. (ed.), *Rural Protest: Peasant Movements and Social Change*, London, Macmillan, 1974.

McAnany, Emile G. (ed.), *Communications in the Rural Third World: The Role of Information in Development*, New York, Praeger, 1981.

Misch, Marion Ruth and Joseph B. Margolin, *Rural Women's Groups as Potential Change Agents: A Study of Columbia, Korea and the Philippines*, Washington, D.C., George Washington University, 1975.

Moore, M.P., "Social Structure and Institutional Performance: Local Farmers' Organisations in Sri Lanka," *Journal of Administration Overseas*, vol. 18, no. 4, October 1979, pp. 240–49.

Narayanasamy, C. et al., *Rural Organisations and Rural Development in Selected Sri Lankan Villages*, Kuala Lumpur, UN Asian and Pacific Development Administration Centre, 1977.

Nash, Manning, *Peasant Citizens: Politics, Religion, and Modernization in Kelantan, Malaysia*, Ohio, Centre for International Studies, Ohio University, 1977.

Park, Chung-Hee, *Saemaul: Korea's New Community Movement*, Seoul, Secretariat of the President, 1979.

"Participation of the Rural Poor in Development," *Development: Seeds of Change*, vol. 1, 1981, pp. 3–67.

Rahman, Anisur, "Mobilization Without Tears: A Conceptual Discussion of Self-reliance Development," in Johan Galtung, Peter O'Brien and Roy Preiswerk (eds), *Self-reliance: A Strategy for Development*, London, Bogle L'Ouverture, 1980, pp. 80–97.

Regional Workshop on the Methods and Techniques of Promoting People's Participation in Local Development [Manila, Dec. 1–8, 1977], Manila, Social Welfare and Development Centre for Asia and the Pacific, 1977.

de Silva, V.S. et al., Bhoomi Sena: A Struggle for People's Power, *Development Dialogue*, vol. 2, 1979, pp. 3–70.

Simpas, Santiago S., "The Role of Local Elites: The Philippine Experience," *Philippine Journal of Public Administration*, vol. 19, nos 1/2, 1975, pp. 63–83.

Smith, David Horton, "Volunteers, Voluntary Associations and Development," *International Journal of Comparative Sociology*, vol. 21, nos 3/4, September–December, 1980.

United Nations, *Popular Participation as a Strategy for Promoting Community-level Action and National Development: Report of the Meeting of the Ad Hoc*

Group of Experts held at UN Headquarters from 23–26 May 1978, New York, 1981.

————, *Popular Participation in Development: Emerging Trends in Community Development*, New York, 1971.

————, *Popular Participation in Decision-making for Development*. New York, 1975.

Waddimba, J., *Some Participative Aspects of Programmes to Involve the Poor in Development*, Geneva, UN Research Institute for Social Development, 1979.

Workshop on Review and Development of Conscientization-Mobilization: Strategies, Methods, Materials, Bangkok, 17–23 March 1980.

Religion and Development

Abdul-Rauf, M., *The Islamic Doctrine of Economics and Contemporary Economic Thought*, Washington, D.C., American Enterprise Institute for Public Policy Research, 1979.

Ahmad, A. (ed.), *Religion and Society in South Asia*, Leiden, E.J. Brill, 1971.

Ahmad, Kurshid, *Islam and the West*, Chicago, Kazi Pub., (n.d.).

Ariyaratne, A.T., *The Religious and Traditional Values in Development in the 80s with Specific Reference to the Sarvodaya Movement (Sri Lanka)*, Colombo, Sarvodaya Institute (n.d.).

Bellah, Robert N., *Beyond Belief: Essays on Religion in a Post-Traditional World*. New York, Harper and Row, 1970.

————, "Reflections on the Protestant Ethic Analogy in Asia," *Journal of Social Issues*, vol. 19, January 1963, pp. 52–60.

————, *Religion and Progress in Modern Asia*, New York, The Free Press, 1965.

————, *Tokugawa Religion: The Values of Preindustrial Japan*, Boston, Beacon Press, 1970.

Bellah, Robert N. and Phillip E. Hammond, *Varieties of Civil Religion*, New York, Harper and Row, 1980.

Bruneau, Thomas C., "The Catholic Church and Development in Latin America: The Role of the Basic Christian Communities," *World Development*, vol. 8, nos 7/8, July/August 1980, pp. 535–44.

Cropland, Ian, "Islam and Political Mobilization in Kashmir, 1931–1934," *Pacific Affairs*, vol. 54, no. 2, Summer 1981, pp. 228–59.

Dfanner, D. and J. Ingersoll, "Theravada Buddhism and Village Economic Behaviour," *Journal of Asian Studies*, vol. 21, no. 3, May 1962.

Dube, S.C., "Traditional Views of Change and Development," in *Absolute Values and the Search for the Peace of Mankind*, New York, The International Cultural Foundation Press, 1980, vol. 1, pp. 277–300.

Dupree, L., "The Political Uses of Religion: Afghanistan," in K.H. Silvert (ed.), *Churches and States; The Religious Institution and Modernization*, New York, American Universities Field Staff, 1967, pp. 195–214.

Esposito, John L. (ed.), *Islam and Development: Religion and Sociopolitical Change*, New York, Syracuse University Press, 1980.

Fischer, Michael M.J., "Islam and the Revolt of the Petit Bourgeoisie," *Daedalus*, Winter 1982, pp. 101–25.

Geertz, C., *Islam Observed: Religious Development in Morocco and Indonesia*, New Haven, Yale University Press, 1968.

Goulet, Denis, "Development Experts: The One-eyed Giants," *World Development*, vol. 8, nos 7/8, July–August 1980, pp. 481–89.

————, *A New Moral Order*, Mary Knoll, Orbis Books, 1974.

Gremillion, J. and W. Ryan (eds), *World Faiths and the New World Order*, Washington, D.C., Inter-religious Peace Colloquium, 1978.

ILO, *Islam and a New International Economic Order: The Social Dimension*, Geneva, 1980.

Ling, Trevor, "Buddhist Values and Development Problems: A Case Study of Sri Lanka," *World Development*, vol. 8, nos 7/8, July–August 1980, pp. 577–86.

Morris, Cynthia Taft and Irma Adelman, "The Religious Factor in Economic Development," *World Development*, vol. 8, nos 7/8, July–August 1980, pp. 491–501.

Norbeck, Edward, *Religion and Society in Modern Japan; Continuity and Change*, Houston, Texas, Rice University, 1970.

"New Religious Consciousness and the Crisis of Modernity," in C.Y. Glock and R.N. Bellah (eds), *The New Religious Consciousness*, Berkeley, University of California Press, 1976, chap. 15.

Pakinson, B., "Non-economic Factors in the Economic Retardation of the Rural Malays," *Modern Asian Studies*, 1967, pp. 40–41.

Ragab, Ibrahim A., Islam and Development, *World Development*, vol. 8, nos 7/8, July–August 1980, pp. 513–21.

Samuelsson, K., *Religion and Economic Action*, New York, Harper and Row, 1961.

Seminar on Religion and Development in Asian Societies, Kandy, 9–16 December 1973, Colombo, Marga Publications, 1974.

Smith, Donald E., *Religion, Politics and Social Change in the Third World*, New York, Free Press, 1971.

Spencer, R.F., *Religion and Change in Contemporary Asia*, Minneapolis, University of Minnesota Press, 1971.

Spiro, M.E., *Buddhism and Society*, New York, Harper and Row, 1970.

Sutcliffe, C.R., " 'Is Islam an Obstacle to Development?' Ideal Patterns of Belief versus Actual Patterns of Behaviour," *Journal of Developing Areas*, vol. 10, October 1975, pp. 77–82.

Tipton, Steven M., "The Moral Logic of Alternative Religions," *Daedalus*, Winter 1982, pp. 185–213.

Von der Mehden, Fred R., "Religion and Development in South-east Asia: A Comparative Study," *World Development*, vol. 8, nos 7/8, July–August 1980, pp. 545–53.

Weber, Max, *The Sociology of Religion*, Trans. by E. Fischolf, Boston, Beacon Press, 1963.

————, *The Protestant Ethic and the Spirit of Capitalism*, New York, Charles Scribner, 1958.

Wilber, Charles K. and Kenneth P. Jameson, "Religious Values and Social Limits to Development," *World Development*, vol. 8, nos. 7/8, July–August 1980, pp. 467–79.

The North-South Dialogue

Al-Sabah, Ali Khalifa, "North-South Dialogue: Impasse and/or Revival," *OPEC Bulletin*, vol. 11, October 1980, pp. 20–25.
Anell, Lavs, "An Equitable World Order," *International Development Review*, vol. 22, nos 2/3, 1980, pp. 84–92.
Balassa, Bela, *Adjustment to External Shocks in Development Economies*, Washington, D.C., World Bank, 1981.
————, *World Trade and the International Economy: Trends, Prospects and Policies*, Washington, D.C., World Bank, 1978.
Brown, Lester R., *World Without Borders*, New York, Vintage Books, 1972.
Corea, Gamani, "The Debt Problems of Developing Countries," *Journal of Development Planning*, vol. 9, 1976, pp. 53–78.
————, *The Instability of an Export Economy*, Colombo, Marga Institute, 1975.
Diwan, Romesh K. and D. Livingston, *Alternative Development Strategies and Appropriate Technology: Science Policy for an Equitable World Order*, New York, Pergamon Press, 1979.
Dorner, Peter and Mahmoud A. El-Shafie (eds), *Resources and Development: Natural Resources Policies and Economic Development in an Interdependent World*, Wisconsin, University of Wisconsin Press, 1980.
Ensminger, Douglas and Paul Boman, *Conquest of World Hunger and Poverty*, Ames, Iowa, Iowa State University Press, 1980.
Erb, Guy F., "The Developing World's 'Challenge' in Perspective," in Guy F. Erb and Valeriana Kallab (eds), *Beyond Dependency: The Developing World Speaks Out*, Washington, D.C., Overseas Development Council, 1975, pp. 135–56.
Finger, J.M., *Industrial Country Policy and Adjustment to Imports from Developing Countries*, Washington, D.C., World Bank, 1981.
Grewlich, Klaus W., *Transnational Enterprises in a New International System*, The Hague, Sijthoff International, 1980.
Hann, Daniel P., "Perspectives on the Future of the World Economy: The Energy Situation and the New International Economic Order," *Economic Forum*, vol. 11, Winter 1980–81, pp. 101–08.
Hansen, Roger D., *Beyond the North-South Stalemate*, New York, McGraw-Hill, 1979.
————, *The US and World Development: Agenda for Action 1976*, New York, Praeger, 1976.
Haq, Khadija (ed.), *Beyond the Brandt Commission*, Washington, D.C., North-South Round Table Secretariat, Society for International Development, 1981.
————, *Dialogue for a New Order*, Oxford, Pergamon Press, 1980.
————, (ed.), *A Global Agenda for the Eighties*, Washington, D.C., North-South Round Table, 1981.
Haq, Mahbub Ul, "Negotiating a New Bargain with the Rich Countries," in Guy F. Erb and Valeriana Kallab (eds), *Beyond Dependency: The Developing World Speaks Out*, Washington, D.C., Overseas Development Council, 1975, pp. 157–64.
————, "Negotiating the Future," *Foreign Affairs*, vol. 59, Winter 1980–81, pp. 398–417.

Hathaway, Dale E., "Food Issues in North-South Relations," *World Economy*, vol. 3, January 1981, 447–59.

Helleiner, Gerald K., *International Economic Disorder: Essays in North-South Relations*, London, Macmillan, 1980.

Howe, James W. and James J. Tarrant, *An Alternative Road to the Post-petroleum Era: North-South Cooperation*, London, Overseas Development Council, 1980.

Larosiere, Jacques de, "Toward a Solution of International Economic Problems," *Finance and Development*, vol. 16, no. 3, September 1979, pp. 12–14.

Lewis, John P., "Aid Issues – 1981 and Beyond," *OECD Observer*, vol. 113, November 1981, pp. 4–9.

North-South: A Programme for Survival, The Report of the Independent Commission on International Development Issues under the Chairmanship of Willy Brandt, London, Pan, 1980.

"North-South Technology Transfer," *OECD Observer*, March 1981, pp. 3–11.

Ramesh, Jairam and Charles Weiss (eds), *Mobilizing Technology for World Development*, New York, Praeger, 1979.

"Reflections on the 'Mutual Interest' Thesis and the Impasse in North-South Negotiations," *Trade and Development*, Autumn 1980, pp. 1–48.

Rich and Poor Nations in the World Economy, New York, McGraw-Hill, 1980.

Sauvant, Karl P. (ed.), *Changing Priorities on the International Agenda: The New International Economic Order*, New York, Pergamon, 1981.

Sauvant, Karl P., *The Group of 77: Evolution, Structure, Organization*, New York, Oceania, 1981.

Sengupta, Arjun, "Issues in the North-South Negotiations on Commodities," *ODI Review*, vol. 2, 1979, pp. 72–86.

Soedjatmoko, *Global Transformation: Search for New Understanding*, Uppsala, Uppsala University, 1981.

United Nations Trade and Development Board, *Restructuring the International Economic Framework: Report by the Secretary-General of the UNCTAD to the Fifth Session of the Conference* [Manila, May 7–June 1, 1979], New York, United Nations, 1980.

Ward, Barbara, "Another Chance for the North?" *Foreign Affairs*, vol. 59, Winter 1980–81, pp. 386–97.

———, "Where There is no Vision, the People Perish," *International Development Review*, vol. 22, no. 4, 1980, pp. 4–8.

Wriggins, W. Havard and Gunnar Adler Karlsson, *Reducing Global Inequities*, New York, McGraw-Hill, 1978.

Management of Social Change

Banks, David J. (ed.), *Changing Identities in Modern Southeast Asia*, The Hague, Mouton, 1976.

Basil, Douglas C. and Curtis W. Cook, *The Management of Change*, London, McGraw-Hill, 1974.

Bennis, Warren G. et al., *The Planning of Change* (2nd. ed.), New York, Holt, Rinehart and Winston, 1969.

Braibanti, Ralph and Joseph J. Spengler, *Tradition, Values, and Socio-economic Development*, Durham, NC, Duke University Press, 1961.

Chu, Godwin C., *Radical Change Through Communication in Mao's China*, Hawaii, East-West Centre Book, 1977.

Dube, S.C., *Explanation and Management of Change*, New York, McGraw-Hill, 1974.

————, *India's Changing Villages: Human Factors in Community Development*, London, Routledge and Kegan Paul, 1958.

Eisenstadt, Shmuel Naoh, *Modernization: Protest and Change*, Englewood Cliffs, Prentice-Hall, 1966.

Etzioni, Amitai and Eva Etzioni, *Social Change: Sources, Patterns and Consequences*, New York, Basic Books, 1964.

Fallers, Lloyd A., *Inequality: Social Stratification Reconsidered*, Chicago, University of Chicago Press, 1973.

Hall, Edward T., *Beyond Culture*, New York, Anchor Books, 1977.

Hernes, Gudmund, "Structural Change in Social Processes," *American Journal of Sociology*, vol. 82, no. 3, November 1976, pp. 513–47.

Hirsch, Fred, *Social Limits to Growth*, London, Routledge and Kegan Paul, 1977.

Hussein, Alatas Syed, *Modernization and Social Change: Studies in Modernization, Religion, Social Change and Development in South-East Asia*, London, Angus and Robertson, 1972.

Jantsch, Erich, *Technological Planning and Social Futures*, London, Associated Business Programmes, 1972.

Kahn, Herman, *World Economic Development 1979 and Beyond*, Boulder, Westview Press, 1979.

Knall, Bruno, "People's Participation in Development," *Local Government and Rural Development Review*, vol. 1, no. 2, April–June 1979, pp. 88–98.

Kothari, Rajni, *Democratic Policy and Social Change in India: Crisis and Opportunities*, Columbia, South Asia Books, 1976.

————, *Environment and Alternative Development*, New York, Institute for World Order, 1981.

————, *Footsteps into the Future: Diagnosis of the Present World and a Design for an Alternative*, Amsterdam, North-Holland, 1974.

Landsberger, Henry A. (ed.), *Rural Protest: Peasant Movements and Social Change*, London, Macmillan, 1974.

Laszlo, Ervin, *A Strategy for the Future: The Systems Approach to World Order*, New York, George Braziller, 1974.

Mann, R.S., *Social Structure, Social Change and Future Trends; Indian Village Perspective*, Jaipur, Rawat Publications, 1979.

Nash, Manning, *Peasant Citizens: Politics, Religion, and Modernization in Kelantan, Malaysia*, Ohio, Centre for International Studies, Ohio University, 1977.

Paiva, J.F.X., "A Conception of Social Development," *Social Science Review*, June, 1977, pp. 327–36.

Pajestka, Josef, "Social Dimensions of Development," in *The Case for Development: Six Studies* by the United Nations Centre for Economic and Social Information, New York, Praeger, 1973.

Simmons, Alan et al., *Social Change and Internal Migration: A Review of*

Research Findings from Africa, Asia, and Latin America, Ottawa, International Development Research Centre, 1977.

Sinai, I. Robert, *The Challenge of Modernization: The West's Impact on the Non-western World*, New York, W.W. Norton, 1964.

Strumpel, Burkhard, *Economic Means for Human Needs: Social Indicators of Well-being and Discontent*, Ann Arbor, Survey Research Centre, Institute for Social Research, University of Michigan, 1976.

Alternatives for Future

Amin, Samir,   "An Alternative Strategy for Development: Industrialisation in the Service of Agriculture," *Ceres*, vol. 14, no. 5, September–October 1981, pp. 27–32.

Arnold, Steven H. and Denis Goulet,   "The Abundant Society and World Order: Alternative Life-style in the US," *Alternatives: A Journal of World Policy*, vol. 5, no. 2, August 1979.

Brown, Lester R.,   *Building a Sustainable Society*, New York, W.W. Norton, 1981.

Development Choices for the 1980s and Beyond [papers presented at the 16th World Conference of the Society for International Development, Colombo, August 13–15, 1979], *International Development Review*, vol. 22, nos. 2/3, 1980, pp. 3–125.

Diwan, Ramesh K. and Dennis Livingston,   *Alternative Development Strategies and Appropriate Technology: Science Policy for an Equitable World Order*, Oxford, Pergamon, 1979.

Falk, Richard A.,   *A Study of Future Worlds*, New York, Free Press, 1975.

Galtung, Johan,   *The True Worlds: A Transnational Perspective*, New York, The Free Press, 1980.

Galtung, Johan, Peter O'Brien and Roy Preiswerk,   *Self-reliance: A Strategy for Development*, London, Bogle L'Ouverture, 1980.

Giarini, Orio,   *Dialogue on Wealth and Welfare: An Alternative View of World Capital Formation*, A Report to the Club of Rome, Oxford, Pergamon Press, 1980.

The Global 2000 Report to the President, A report prepared by the Council on Environmental Quality and the Department of State, Washington, D.C., 1981.

Hawrylyshyn, Bohdan,   *Road Maps to the Future; Towards more Effective Societies*, Oxford, Pergamon Press, 1980.

Henderson, Hazel,   *Creating Alternative Futures*, London, Putnam, 1978.

Howe, James W. and James J. Tarrant,   *An Alternative Road to the Post-petroleum Era: North-South Cooperation*, Washington, D.C., Overseas Development Council, 1980.

Kothari, Rajni, "Environment and Alternative Development," *Alternatives: A Journal of World Policy*, vol. 5, no. 4, January 1980.

――――――, *Footsteps into the Future: Diagnosis of the Present World and a Design for an Alternative*, Amsterdam, North-Holland, 1974.

――――――, "Towards a Just World," *Alternatives: A Journal of World Policy*, vol. 5, no. 1, 1979, pp. 1–42.

Kuitenbrouwer, J.B.W.,   *Towards Self-reliant Integrated Development*, The Hague, Institute of Social Studies, 1975.

Lagos, Gustavo and Horacio H. Godoy, *Revolution of Being: A Latin American View of the Future*, New York, Free Press, 1977.

Laszlo, Ervin (ed.), *Goals for Mankind; A Report to the Club of Rome*, London, Macmillan, 1977.

Leontief, Wassily, Ann P. Carter and Peter A. Petri, *Future of the World Economy; A United Nations Study*, New York, Oxford University Press, 1977.

Lopez, Salvador P. *Development Alternatives for the Third World*, Los Banos, University of the Philippines, 1980.

Marois, M. (ed.), *Towards a Plan of Action for Mankind: Problems and Perspectives*, Amsterdam, North-Holland, 1974.

Matthews, William H. (ed.), *Outer Limits and Human Needs: Resource and Environmental Issues of Development Strategy*, Uppsala, The Dag Hammarskjold Foundation, 1976.

Meadows, Dennis, *A Search for Sustainable Futures*, Cambridge, MA, Ballinger, 1977.

Meadows, Donella H. et al., *The Limits to Growth; A Report for the Club of Rome's Project on the Predicament of Mankind*, New York, Universe Books, 1974.

Mendlovitz, Saul H. (ed.), *On the Creation of a Just World Order: Preferred Worlds for the 1990s*, Amsterdam, North-Holland, 1974.

Mesarovic, Mihajlo and Eduard Pestel, *Mankind at the Turning Point: The Second Report to the Club of Rome*, New York, E.P. Dutton, 1974.

Mittleman, James H., "Alternative to Conventional Strategies for Development: Mozambique Experience," *Alternatives: A Journal of World Policy*, vol. 5. no. 3, November 1979.

Nerfin, Marc (ed.), *Another Development: Approaches and Strategies*, Uppsala, Dag Hammarskjold Foundation, 1977.

Organisation for Economic Co-operation and Development, *Interfutures; Facing the Future: Mastering the Probable and Managing the Unpredictable*, Paris, 1979.

Parthasarathi, Ashok, *The Role of Self-reliance in Alternative Strategies for Development*, Paper presented to the 25th Pugwash Conference, Madras, 13–19 January 1976.

Rist, Gilbert, "Alternative Strategies to Development," *International Development Review*, vol. 22, nos 2/3, 1980, pp. 102–15.

Seers, Dudley, *Alternative Scenarios for Developing Countries; The Fundamental Issues*, Brighton, Institute for Development Studies, 1977.

Seneviratne, Gamini, *Economic Cooperation Among Developing Countries; New Dimensions in the Thrust of Collective Self-reliance*, New York, United Nations, 1980.

Senghass, Dieter, "Dissociation and Autocentric Development: An Alternative Development Policy for the Third World," *Economics*, vol. 18, 1978, pp. 7–42.

Spekke, Andrew A. (ed.), *The Next 25 Years: Crisis and Opportunity*, Washington, D.C., World Future Society, 1975.

Toffler, Alvin, *The Third Wave*, New York, Bantam Books, 1980.

Tugwell, Franklin, *Search for Alternatives: Public Policy and the Study of the Future*, Cambridge, MA, Winthrop, 1973.

United Nations Department of International Economic and Social Affairs, *Interrelations: Resources, Environment, Population and Development*,

Proceedings of a United Nations Symposium held at Stockholm from 6–10 August, 1979, New York, 1980.

What Now: Another Development, The 1975 Dag Hammarskjold report on development and international cooperation, Uppsala, 1975.

Index